Fidel Castro's Agricultural Follies

Absurdity, Waste and Parasitism

JOSÉ ÁLVAREZ, PH.D.

ISBN: 0988914263
ISBN 13: 9780988914261
Library of Congress Control Number: 2014914042
Jose Alvarez, Wellington, FL

Acclaims

In this book, José Álvarez combines his long career as an expert on Cuban agriculture and an even longer career observing, studying--and during the 1960s--enduring Cuba's failed policies and Fidel Castro's authoritarian, I-know-best, ruling style. It is thoroughly researched, written in exquisite prose, and sprinkled with the characteristic irony and irreverent humor of the Cuban intellectual. At times, readers will find themselves in García Márquez's hallucinating Macondo or in Vargas Llosa's unforgiving Peruvian jungle; but this is not a book of fiction.

Luis Martínez-Fernández, Professor of History at the University of
Central Florida; and author of *Revolutionary Cuba* (University Press
of Florida, 2014).

In choosing Cuba's disastrous experience with agriculture to illustrate some of Fidel Castro's bizarre delusions, José Álvarez has found a novel way to tell the familiar story of the failure of Castroism. Fidel's agricultural follies would be a more amusing tale had they not yielded a harvest of scarcity and hunger for the Cuban people.

Tom Gjelten, author of *Bacardi and the Long Fight for Cuba:*
The Biography of a Cause (Viking, 2008).

Dr. Álvarez rightfully points out that the Soviet Union and other communist/centrally-planned economies have failed at controlled mass agriculture efforts because they neither recognize, nor want to allow, site specific agricultural management that is necessary to allow for maximizing production from the optimization of the local soil, environment and biological resources. Dr. Álvarez's book is insightful across a broad scale of political, cultural and economic aspects. Aspiring politicians, leaders, and anyone with an interest in understanding Cuba or other attempts at such totalitarian governments will benefit from reading it.

Zane R. Helsel, Professor and Extension Specialist in
Agriculture Energy at Rutgers University; and a life member of the
American Society of Agricultural and Biological Engineers.

In this appraisal of socialist Cuba's economic development, Dr. Álvarez shows how and why Fidel Castro's unbridled megalomania devastated the country's political economy and stifled its social progress. The interconnectedness of charismatic rule, narcissistic personal traits and autocratic decision-making form the pathological matrix defining Fidel Castro's behavior. As the cause of colossal blunders and irreversible damage to the economy and social system, that matrix drove Castro's wretched choices and ignorant decisions while the arrogant leader exercised direct power. And Dr. Álvarez properly attributes Cuba's economic ruin and descent into insolvency and mendicancy to Fidel Castro's quixotic fixation with himself.

Juan M. del Águila, Retired Associate Professor of Political Sciences
at Emory University and author of *Cuba: Dilemmas of a Revolution*
(Westview Press, 1994).

This book by one of the world's experts on Cuban agriculture has an amazing amount of information, but Álvarez manages to make it extremely interesting and with frequent touches of humor. It is a wonderful reading, which I recommend for experts and the general public alike.

Carmelo Mesa-Lago, Distinguished Service Professor Emeritus of Economics
and Latin American Studies at the University of Pittsburgh and author of
numerous books on Cuba.

Most people regard Fidel Castro either as a great revolutionary or a bloody dictator. Few know him as a world-class crackpot inventor and frustrated would-be scientist whose madcap ideas destroyed Cuban agriculture and the island's economy. During his half century in power, Castro experimented with everything from creating a New Cuban Man to cloning his favorite champion milk cow. None of the experiments worked. Now, thanks to José Álvarez, we have an entertaining and encyclopedic history of Castro's hair brained efforts to re-engineer the island. This book is must reading for anybody interested in Cuba.

Jose de Cordoba, Latin America correspondent for

The Wall Street Journal.

Dedicated to
G.B. "Jerry" Hagelberg
(1925 – 2011)

For his rigorous thinking, his humorous pedagogy and,
In addition, his sporadic reprimands.

For the love he and Jeanne always showed
For my family and for Cuba.

It is difficult to imagine him resting in peace…

He had doubts about working on this project.
I hope he was wrong… at least this time!

When I was younger, I lied all the time,
Because once you understand the power of lying,
It is really like magic because you transform reality for people.
Louis Szekely (1967 -)
(Comedian)

About The Cover

The illustration by Virginia Gifford captures the essence of this book, which is to present Fidel Castro as a Cuban Don Quixote. Like Cervantes' character, he sees himself as the valiant knight devoted to fighting the injustices of the world. However, he is a delusional fool like his predecessor.

In dealing with the agricultural sector, the Cuban Quixote showed a whimsical imagination that made him believe that he knew better than the best scientists did. Dressed in an outlandish costume, he rides his Rocinante over a land devastated by soil erosion, wielding a dry sugarcane stalk that represents the failure of his goal of a 10-million-ton harvest. Over the years, he has chosen several Sanchos who all have been cast aside leaving a trail of wise, but discarded, aides in his wake because he could never accept either criticism or advice.

The cow sticking her head inside one of the windmills (silent witnesses of past failures), as if it was another air-conditioning experiment, represents part of his genetic revolution. In the distant background, one can hardly see the smokeless sugar mills not grinding since he decided to restructure Cuba's main source of employment and foreign exchange. The dog observes him passing along in prudent silence, beside the midget cow –humble successor of his beloved "Ubre Blanca" who died before she could supply all Cubans with her milk.

Above all, Fidel Castro's haughty and arrogant face says it all.

This is his story, both a comedy and a tragedy.

TABLE OF CONTENTS

List of Tables and Figures

Tables

Preface and Acknowledgments

The events leading to the writing of this book started in Cuba at the end of 1961 when I realized that the program of the Cuban government was the antithesis of what we had proclaimed during the struggle against the previous dictatorship. My disenchantment made me drop out of Law School, submit my resignation in my place of employment and request permission to leave the country. The latter did not become a reality until early February 1969.

Many things happened during those long years. One of them was my first contact with agriculture and its related activities. The initiation came in the form of a telegram, not the one allowing our departure but one containing the instructions to show up every Sunday in a certain place located less than one hour from my home. About one hundred men performed activities to support the gigantic project Fidel Castro had called "Havana's Green Belt", explained in chapter 7. Months later, the officer in charge of the operation instructed us to gather at 7:00 in the morning, at the corner of Avenida Rancho Boyeros and Calle 100, with our belongings. I suspected an assignment in a very distant place and, since I had problems with my documents, decided not to show up until more than five years later. After the passport, the "agriculture's letter" was perhaps the most important document a man needed to leave the country.

The astonishment of the Immigration officials generated threats of staying forever in the countryside. Because of the revolution's generosity, I was to engross what I call "The Nameless Brigades" in chapter 6, becoming an internal exile in the plains of Camagüey province, more than 300 miles from home. I was lucky. The prediction of the morons at Immigration fell short and, less than four months later, I was flying north with my wife, daughter and aunt. I do not remember how many times I swore not put a foot in an agricultural field let alone study something related with that subject.

During my undergraduate work at the University of Florida, I took two courses in the agricultural economics department to realize their importance in the development field. My contempt had disappeared. During my years in graduate school, I became interested in Cuban agriculture and wrote a couple of papers. After graduating with a Ph.D. in food and resource economics, I became an assistant professor in my Department at the Research and Education Center in Belle Glade, Florida. I still do not believe I turned down a position on the main campus to return to the countryside.

For the next 30 years, I devoted a great deal of my time to learn more about Cuba's agricultural sector. My list of publications includes several of its components. I even obtained several grants and was able to pay several professional visits to the island. I was happy with my research and writing but could not forget Havana's green belt and the nameless brigades. I had already added a few more of the so-called "Fidel's Special Plans" to my collection, even though there was not much information about them. When my book *Cuba's agricultural sector* (University Press of Florida) came out in 2004, it contained an Appendix entitled "Plans, projects and pesos" with brief discussions of several of the crazy projects of the Commander in chief.

That process continued. I was just waiting for the right moment to finish the writing and publish the findings of my long research. The material I had compiled and analyzed should become available to the public.

The time finally came to make an inventory and evaluate Castro's agricultural follies. On July 31, 2006 Vice-President Raúl Castro assumed the duties of President of Cuba's Council of State in a temporary transfer of power due to Fidel Castro's illness. On February 24, 2008 the National Assembly of People's Power unanimously chose General Raúl Castro as his brother's permanent successor. Although Fidel Castro has partially recovered, he will not resume his former duties. His complete control over the economy —especially the agricultural sector's—during nearly fifty years ended with his illness.

The time has come for this book to tell the truth. Its title, *Fidel Castro's agricultural follies: absurdity, waste and parasitism*, determines its organization. Part I deals with the absurdity. Four chapters look into Castro's promises and predictions that never materialized, followed by a discussion on leadership theory and Castro's decision-making style. The long search for an economic model is then discussed. The last chapter of this section presents the facts of agricultural performance during his tenure and the three alleged culprits he blames for his failures. Part II encompasses seven chapters that describe and analyze some of his projects including the obsession for labor mobilizations, the preference for giant projects, and a discussion of management exceptionalism. Part III covers the parasitism. It is an attempt at answering the question: where did Castro obtain the resources? The main sources are listed and quantified. The process started with the recovering of assets misappropriated during the Batista dictatorship, followed by the expropriation of assets belonging to national and foreign individuals and corporations. The urban housing, the industrial and banking sectors were the next targets. Then, the regime made a currency exchange. Finally, the last vestiges of private property fell in state's hands in 1968 during a so-called "revolutionary offensive". Borrowing was also an important source of funding and this section quantifies the case of the Soviet Union and western countries. Hubbard and Duggan gave some thoughts to the forgiveness of large parts of foreign debt, which they call another form of charity in *The aid trap*. Such process would allow the Raúl Castro regime to start the cycle all over again. The recent emphasis on lifting whatever remains of the United States economic embargo seems to indicate that the regime could be looking at the Export-Import Bank to finance future purchases. In case of default (as has been the case before) the American taxpayer would be subsidizing a regime that in more than five decades has been unable to provide higher output and human satisfaction to its people. These pages seem to indicate that the Castro regime never intended to solve the problems. The current process of reforms initiated by Raúl Castro, although not part of Fidel's delusions, is an attempt at showing that the Cuban regime is changing as if Raúl was different.

Many people are using those mild reforms as the reason to declare, "This time is different," as stated in the book written by Reinhart and Rogoff when studying

José Álvarez, Ph.D.

800 years of financial folly. There are only two scenarios when the statement would become a reality. The first would be that Cuba pays its debts. The second would portray a successful process of Raúl Castro's reforms. In this case, despite the possibility of paying, it would not be enough. As it has been recently expressed in Venezuela in an article written by María Corina Machado, "the issue is not to better the condition of captivity, but to live in freedom". I believe that the probabilities for both scenarios are slim. If the opportunity arises, this time will be the same. Cuba's past behavior, current economic conditions and the nature of the regime testify to that fact.

Rather than increasing the volume of this book, I decided to post some of the information on the book's website (www.cubanquixote.com). That includes the list of abbreviations, list of common and scientific names, Tables about costs and quantities of different projects, and some illustrations.

Numerous persons and institutions have contributed to my studying of Cuban agriculture since my interest on the subject arose in the early-1970s. I want to thank all of them.

Recent collaborations include those of Francisco J. Proenza, Juan Tomás Sánchez, Luis Domínguez and Ricardo Vega. My gratitude to Kate Clifford, of Canada' _Holstein Journal,_ who not only provided permission to reproduce the photo of "Rosafe Signet" she sent me, but researched other topics. I owe special thanks to my brother Fernando Álvarez and his wife Sharon Gifford, who offered useful suggestions for key sections, becoming vigilant reviewers at almost every stage of the project. Jorge F. Pérez-López had the patience to read and make corrections to an entire early version. His criticisms and recommendations improved substantially the wording and message of this book. Juan M. del Águila did the same with two chapters. The peculiar cover is the product of Virginia Gifford's creative abilities and I want to give her special thanks.

José Álvarez
Wellington, Florida
Summer 2014

Introduction

Despite the fact that this book contains numerous footnotes, an extensive bibliography, tables and charts, it is not a scholarly publication. It could not be because the real author is Fidel Castro, the Cuban Quixote. Delusional fools do not generate materials for academic books. I organized his projects, selected quotes from his speeches and found data to demonstrate that almost all of them were follies. When faced with such a task, it is very difficult to escape the temptation of using a little Cuban humor. It could not be otherwise. Fidel Castro promised to take Cuba to the top place on this planet. He predicted producing more citrus, fish and other commodities than the United States, more irrigation than the Aswan dam, more citrus than Israel, more milk than Holland, and more everything than the rest of the world, By doing so, he was making fun of his people and the rest of the world. He was offending our intelligence. He was exposing himself to ridicule and scorn. For all those reasons, one cannot write a scholarly piece about his deeds, especially about his destruction of Cuba's agriculture.

Don Quixote de Birán exercised absolute power over Cuba's agricultural sector. He did so through the so-called "Fidel's Special Plans.". These pages reveal the degree of delusional foolishness shared by Don Quixote de la Mancha and the Cuban leader. Almost all projects were failed follies financed first by several means of expropriation and then by borrowing with no apparent intention of paying back. Soviet subsidies and loans from western countries helped him in his plans.

Rather than explaining the content of the book in this Introduction, I want to describe for the reader the environment surrounding Castro's follies. Why did they happen in the first place? The foreign photojournalist Lee Lockwood asked him in 1965 why he devoted so much of his time to agriculture. The question arose from Castro's complaining about his lack of a technical education that had forced him to acquire a basic knowledge of agriculture. His question should have been, "why must a head of State become the unchallenged decision-maker of the agricultural sector?"

It is difficult not to acknowledge Castro's masterful political adroitness, more than demonstrated during his 50 years in power, turning defeats into victories like in the Mariel exodus and the 10-million-sugar ton harvest, and in his relations with the United States and the Soviet Union. However, most of his agricultural projects failed, and the blame rests squarely on his shoulders. What accounts for the dismal performance of the projects described in this book?

There are two possible answers. The first deals with Castro's personality traits and the second resides in his management style. In the words of Will Rogers: "What hurts you most is not what you do not know, it is what you think you know, but just ain't so." [*Lo peor no es dejar de saber, sino creer que se* sabe] Despite his confession of ignorance about the process of agriculture, according to French agronomist René Dumont, "Fidel believes he knows everything in several domains much better than the rest. His pride is his worst enemy." Castro always paid attention only to the recommendations he liked. Once he made a decision, criticism was out of the question. Fidel Castro did not allow dissent from his view and seldom followed the advice provided by domestic (he had several Sanchos throughout the years) and foreign advisors when their opinions contradicted his. Dumont stated that Castro believed to be more capable than other people and that "he should acquire a little of the humility of men who are truly great." Too often, people could hear in Cuba: "You're right, but Fidel doesn't agree."

The second answer relates to his management style.

Castro's "command and countermand" style while leading the sugar industry, applies to the entire agricultural sector. Such disastrous leadership has never been recognized, despite the fact that his economic record, as French journalist and writer Serge Raffy defined it, "is one of unbroken failure, and many of the mistakes of previous economic campaigns are being repeated".

Depending on the project, two different approaches or tactics hid those failures. In one, his political skills were able to turn setbacks into victories. When Castro went on radio and television to announce the catastrophic results of the 10-million-ton sugar harvest of 1970, he declared, "The people have won a victory. The people have not lost this battle... and [we must] convert the setback into victory." Reaching the desired production goal became less important than the alleged moral values acquired by the people during the long sugar campaign. An imaginary ideological victory replaced the unfulfilled goal.

The second approach was more typical of bureaucracies everywhere. There was never a report about discarded projects. The results of these failures have been more perverse in Cuba, because there never was a political opposition to contest them or the leader(s) who launched and managed them. The Cuban writer Hugo Luis Sánchez describes how it is done in his short story titled "Dulce hogar" [Sweet home]: "Anyone can say the day [a project] started, but nobody the day it was ended, or if it was a success or a failure. It languishes in the memory hoping that forgetfulness takes care of it."

In order to maintain absolute power, the Cuban regime has exerted complete control over society by means of a ruined economy, and a divided society completely dependent on the State. The situation, according to Raffy, has produced a new literary gender: "tragic unrealism." This book, despite its touch of humor, appears to belong in that category and hopes to generate enthusiasm to continue this enormous task. Some scholars, like Haroldo Dilla, have shown interest in knowing the cost of Castro's agricultural follies. He hopes that, in the future, some economic historian will compute their cost, "Probably that is when we may perceive the magnitude of the damage caused by the … many ideas turned into unchallenged policies."

As expected, the Cuban Quixote never left his imaginary world. During the 100 hours of conversation with Ignacio Ramonet, he confessed: "I've made mistakes, but none of them were strategic – just tactical. A person regrets many things, sometimes even in a speech… But I have not one iota of regret about what we've done in our country and the way we've organized our society." The reader should keep in mind that lack of remorse while reading the pages that follow.

One of his obsessions, shared by Ernesto Guevara, was the creation of a new man, present in most parts of the book. "Che" was perhaps his most important Sancho in the ideological area. In his farewell letter of 1965, Guevara reminded Castro of "the pride of belonging to our people in the brilliant yet sad days of the Caribbean crisis." They are proud of having brought the world to the brink of a nuclear catastrophe, which should give the reader an idea of the degree of delusional disorder they shared.

Very few people know about the failure of his obsessive quest. While still in the Sierra Maestra, the Cuban Don Quixote wrote a note to another of his Sanchos, his confidant Celia Sánchez. It was June 5, 1958: "After seeing the rockets fired at Mario's house, I have sworn to myself that the Americans are going to pay dearly for what they are doing. When this war ends, a much longer and bigger war will begin for me: the war that I am going to wage against them. I realize that that will be my true destiny." Well, he lost that war. Today, Cuba is more dependent on the United States than when the Cuban Quixote took power in 1959, as revealed by the large percentage of its population receiving remittances, family packages, and visits from the United States, not counting the huge quantities of U.S. agricultural exports.

While researching and writing about the topic of this book, I felt the need to show the relationship of Cuba's agriculture I was unveiling with the rest of the economic, social and political Cuba. I then recalled a passage attributed to Cervantes. Don Quixote and Sancho Panza are riding when a group of barking dogs comes close to them. Sancho, who is sane, captures the reality of the situation, but Don Quixote, because of the chronic enthusiasm resulting from his madness, says, "¡Sancho, if the dogs bark is because we are moving!"

The Cuban Don Quixote has been riding alone for over half a century. Now and then he has done it in the company of a temporary Sancho. For non-Cuban residents, it is very difficult to understand why he does not find multitudes of barking dogs. He rides along the setting he created and that allowed his failures in the agricultural sector to go uncontested. That milieu is similar to the one described by Vargas Llosa in *The city and the dogs*: closed and oppressive, as the military school of the novel, where the relations among the cadets, and those with their superiors, friends and family are characterized by suspicion (sometimes hate) and helplessness faced with an unfair and seemingly immutable social order. Maybe Castro's chronic delusion prevented him from understanding that the lack of barking is not a sign of approval but a silent warning that he has been riding along the wrong path.

In Cervantes's novel, Don Quixote dies after finally recovering his sanity ("he died sane but lived crazy"). That is unlikely to happen with the Cuban Quixote.

PART I

THE ABSURDITY

Chapter 1

FIDEL CASTRO: THE DISMAL SOOTHSAYER

... these are not promises. Facts, and not promises, are the essence of this revolution.
In addition, usually the facts come before the words.
Fidel Castro[1]

Revolution is never lying or violating ethical principles.
Fidel Castro.[2]

*K*arl Marx believed he had discovered the laws that moved society from one stage to the next. Capitalism had led to the creation of a heavy industrial sector, giving rise to a class struggle between the bourgeoisie and the proletariat that eventually would bring the latter to power via a revolution driven by economics. If that were correct, the first proletarian revolution would have taken place in a country with a heavily industrialized economy. He predicted that the first transition from capitalism to socialism would occur in Germany or England. He was wrong. It happened in Russia: an agrarian economy lacking the strong contradictions between the two classes to incite working people to revolt. Instead of economics, it was politics what produced the first socialist State in the Marxist sense.

---

1   In the inauguration of several hydraulic projects in the Cauto river on May 30, 1968: http://www.cuba.cu/gobierno/discursos/1968/esp/f300568e.html.
2   Speech of May 1, 2000, at http://www.cuba.cu/gobierno/discursos/2000/ing/f010500i.html.

Unlike Marx, and despite his claim that facts would always precede his promises, Fidel Castro made dozens of promises and predictions that never materialized. This chapter presents a selection of them arranged under seven topics in chronological order and followed by the facts that refute them. The contents of this chapter seem to indicate that Fidel Castro had a problem with semantics, his crystal ball needed a thorough cleaning or those promises and predictions were the result of his delusions about his alleged monopoly of knowledge.

Never Less than Number One

Fidel Castro was always obsessed with being at the top. Once in power, he saw Cuba as a narcissistic extension of himself. The dream of making Cuba the number one country in many areas was present early in the revolution. His first prediction in that regard set the first Olympian record of optimism. On February 16, 1959, he predicted:[3]

> I estimate that, **in the next few years**, Cuba's standard of living –if
> the plans continue and we are not tripped—will be higher than in the
> United States and Russia. [We] will increase five-fold the living standard.

Later that day he repeated the prediction during the swearing in ceremony as Prime Minister, expanding even more the expected record: "we will achieve a standard of living **higher than any other country in the world.**"[4]

The key words in the first are "in the next few years" and in the second, "higher than any other country in the world." Obviously, Fidel Castro had a problem with the branch of mathematics called "order theory,"[5] which investigates our intuitive notion of order using binary relations. Relative rankings and positions use the format framework it provides.

The top ranking did not materialize for the simple reason that, as Castro has confessed repeatedly, he had already planned the establishment of a socialist society in Cuba and none of the socialist countries was ever at the top of that list.

---

3 At a meeting with members of the Association of Cuban Architects: http://www.cuba.cu/
gobierno/discursos/1959/esp/c160259e.html.

4 http://www.cuba.cu/gobierno/discursos/1959/esp/c160259e.html.

5 http://en.wikipedia.org/wiki/Order_theory.

The Human Development Index of the United Nations for 2011 gave Cuba[6] a ranking of 59, while The Russian Federation[7] placed 55th and the United States[8] was number three.

On October 19, 1959, during a meeting with members of the banking sector, Castro predicted another first place for Cuba, surpassing again the United States.[9] According to him, the U.S. were behind in reproducing river fish. Cuba was finishing a breeding center to raise fish, after studying 540 lagoons. He predicted production of 100 million trouts each year to stock those lagoons, placing Cuba in an advantageous position "over any other country in the world in river fishing issues, because we already have [that position in] sea and maritime fishing."

This time he claimed three first places: river, sea and maritime fishing. Was it possible that, hardly nine months after taking power, the Cuban regime had already "almost completed building" a breeding center for fish raising? What time is necessary to study 540 lagoons? Had they conducted experiments to allow Castro to predict a production of 100 million fish per year?

Despite his magic prediction, at the time of implementing the consumer goods rationing system in 1962, each person received 1 pound of fish per month, increasing later to 2 pounds, then decreasing to 6-9 ounces, and even selling outside the quota system in some years.[10] Since 2012, no fish is available through the rationing system and chicken quotas may take their place in some instances.[11] Perhaps the fish left the safety of the tanks where they lived to migrate to the United States. There is no other plausible explanation for the disappearance of 100 million trouts per year. If harvesting had started in 1960, by the year he resigned as head of the Cuban State, about 48 billion trouts had disappeared!

---

6   http://hdrstats.undp.org/en/countries/profiles/CUB.html.

7   http://hdrstats.undp.org/en/countries/profiles/RUS.html.

8   http://hdrstats.undp.org/en/countries/profiles/USA.html.

9   http://www.cuba.cu/gobierno/discursos/1959/esp/c191059e.html.

10   Álvarez (2004a: 135).

11   http://www.havanatimes.org/?p=83878.

He then went from fish to milk. His prediction of December 12, 1961 brought to mind one famous fable.[12] The country with the highest milk production per cow in the world was the Netherlands, with an average of 21 liters per cow. He then added: "Imagine that by the year 1970 we were milking a million cows, averaging seven liters... [That] would be 7 million liters per day. Havana actually needs half a million. Now, if of the 5 million breeding cows we milked 2 million ...yielding two liters per cow, we would have four million more, 11 million liters of milk. So people can... fill a swimming pool with cow's milk and bathe. Of course, once the demand is satisfied, the milk would be use to make cheese, and butter and dairy products that we do not consume, we would export them!"

Although almost all of his plans and projects deserve mentioning it, this is the place where the Aesop's fable entitled "The milkmaid and her pail"[13] appears more relevant: Patty the Milkmaid was going to market carrying her milk in a pail on her head. While walking, she began to imagine what she would do with the money she would get for the milk. She would buy some fowls and they would lay eggs each morning, and she would sell them, and with that money, she would buy a new dimity frock and a chip hat to attract the attention of all young men. The enthusiasm leads her to toss her head back; the pail fell off it, spilling all the milk, forcing the return home. The mother's advice "Do not count your chickens before they are hatched".

As in most cases, Fidel was counting before the hatching had taken place. In fact, milk-rationing quotas have remained in place at roughly the same level since their establishment in 1962: children under seven, ill persons and the elderly can purchase one liter of fresh milk daily. The rest of the population receives three cans of condensed milk per person per month.[14]

A fundamental difference between the Milkmaid and Fidel Castro is that Castro was never accountable for his decisions and he continued counting imaginary chickens. The previous prediction was not enough for him. Despite the fact

---

12 http://www.cuba.cu/gobierno/discursos/1961/esp/f121261e.html.

13 http://www.umass.edu/aesop/content.php?n=23&i=1.

14 Álvarez (2004a: 135).

that milk rations were in place, on July 12, 1963 he dared to challenge the world leadership position in milk production[15] "... based on the example of Holland, I am absolutely convinced, --and I dare to say it here without fear of talking my head off, and let history judge me for what I'm going to say— that we can get to produce as much milk as Holland... and I say no more."

Well, *Comandante,* history did not need to judge you. The facts did. FAOSTAT (the statistical office of the Food and Agriculture Organization of the United Nations) reports that the Netherlands[16] produced 11,627,312 metric tons of fresh whole cow milk in 2011, while Cuba[17] produced 599,500 metric tons, or 5.16% of Holland's output.

Of all agricultural commodities, citrus was one of Fidel's favorites. Perhaps because of the orange grove his parents planted in their estate in Birán (see chapter 2). The goal he set for Cuba on April 29, 1967 is laughable:[18] "Our goal is to compete with the more advanced countries of the world in productivity per hectare of citrus ... But to get an idea of what will be to have planted 100 000 hectares of citrus, suffice to say that we will produce in a year almost as much citrus as the United States now produces for a population of 200 million."

The United States ranked third in world total citrus production in 2007 with 10 million metric tons (first in grapefruit with 1.580 million). Cuba did not rank among the top 10 producers despite the fact that citrus fruits were among the top priority agricultural crops.[19] In 2007, Cuba ranked 54 in oranges and 30 in grapefruit production.[20]

When Castro made that prediction, he had already discussed the topic with Lee Lockwood, who interviewed him in the summer of 1965.[21] They were in the Isle of Pines, where Castro informed the American photojournalist about the

---

15 http://www.cuba.cu/gobierno/discursos/1963/esp/f200763e.html.

16 http://faostat.fao.org/site/339/default.aspx.

17 http://faostat.fao.org/site/339/default.aspx.

18 http://www.cuba.cu/gobierno/discursos/1967/esp/f290467e.html.

19 http://en.wikipedia.org/wiki/Citrus_production as it appears in FAO, Economic and Social Department, the Statistics Division.

20 http://faostat.fao.org/site/339/default.aspx.

21 Lockwood (1990: 88-89).

plans for the region: "We are going to have an area planted with citrus trees as extensive as all Israel has, and we expect to achieve a yield as high as theirs. It is possible that Cuba's overall national production of citrus fruits will come to triple theirs between 1970 and 1975, when the groves will come into full production. That will make us the leading exporter in the world."

Did Fidel Castro really believe that? The statistics for his prediction years indicate that he was completely out of touch with reality: Cuba's total citrus production in 1975 was 175,206 metric tons, while Israel produced 1,510,100 metric tons the same year.[22] Obviously, Cuba did not triple Israel's production at the end of the 1970-1975 period given by Castro. On the contrary, Israel's output was 8.6 times greater than Cuba's. Needles to say, Cuba has never been the world's leading citrus exporter.

A similar line of reasoning (same acreage and forthcoming larger productivity), reappears on January 6, 1968, as part of his obsession of bettering the state of Florida: "...And if they in Florida have been able to develop a citrus industry in a land worse than ours, and with two enemies [hurricanes and freezes], there is no doubt that we will have a citrus industry superior to Florida's. There is not the least doubt about that."[23]

In 1990, Cuba produced 1.017 million metric tons of citrus.[24] That same crop season, Florida produced 9 million metric tons,[25] despite a severe freeze on December 22-26, 1989.[26] It is interesting to note that, as will be explained in chapter 4, Castro blames hurricanes as one of the culprits for Cuba's low production, while boasts that the island can maintain higher levels of output because of hurricanes and freezes in Florida. As is said in Spanish, "por la boca muere el pez" [fish die by the mouth].

Water works projects were also an obsession of the leader of the revolution. He referred often to them, always making comparisons. The most impacting one

---

22 http://faostat.fao.org/site/567/DesktopDefault.aspx?PageID=567#ancor.

23 http://www.cuba.cu/gobierno/discursos/1968/esp/f060168e.html.

24 From figures provided by CUBAFRUTAS and appearing in several publications.

25 State of Florida Statistical Report CS0102.

26 http://flcitrusmutual.com/render.aspx?p=/industry-issues/weather/freeze_timeline.aspx.

was made on October 30, 1967:[27] "We aspire to irrigate 8,290,000 acres of land, equivalent to twice the [area irrigated by the] Aswan Dam, built in Egypt in one of the largest rivers in the world."

A cursory analysis of the goal to irrigate 8,290,000 acres, twice the Aswan's irrigation capability, shows: 1. That the acreage represents more than 52% of Cuba's agricultural area, since Cuba has 6,405,600 ha,[28] or 15,829,000 acres of agricultural area. 2. Aswan's irrigation capacity is 13,000 square miles, or 8,320,000 acres.[29] The figure is not half of Castro's goal, but an almost identical one!

On January 2, 1968, he mentioned a group of commodities for which Cuba could achieve the leading producer rank. After stating that all knew that "no one can compete on sugar with this country in any sense", he mentioned the others: meat, tropical fruits, citrus, coffee, banana and pinapple.[30]

How accurate were those predictions? World production rankings from FAOSTAT for the year 2011shows Cuba in 54th place in raw centrifugal sugar production;[31] and it is not even ranked among the top on meat production. Tropical crops do not appear among the classifications. It ranks 67 in citrus, 62 in green coffee, 67 in bananas and 56 in pineapple. This is another example of Castro's lack of knowledge of "order theory."

Obsessed as he was with surpassing the United States in everything, he included rice production in his predictions. On May 26, 1969, speaking in the ceremony merging the National Hydraulic Institute with the Agricultural Development Department, he stated that Cuba was on its way to develop a modern rice industry, surpassing per capita productivity in the United States.[32]

---

27 http://www.cuba.cu/gobierno/discursos/1967/esp/f301067e.html.
28 (http://www.one.cu/aec2012/esp/20080618_tabla_cuadro.htm).
29 http://en.wikipedia.org/wiki/Aswan_Dam.
30 http://www.cuba.cu/gobierno/discursos/1968/esp/f020168e.html.
31 http://faostat.fao.org/site/339/default.aspx.
32 http://www.cuba.cu/gobierno/discursos/1969/esp/f260569e.html.

FAOSTAT reports production for 2011 of 566,400 metric tons of paddy rice for Cuba[33] and of 8,388,780 metric tons for the United States[34] for a population of 11,247,925 for Cuba and approximately 311,800,000 for the United States.[35] The resulting per capita production figures are 0.05 for Cuba and 0.027 for the United States. Castro's prediction, however, was in "per capita productivity" and, to calculate that, one needs to know the number of hours worked and I could not find them in any of the statistical reports I checked.

Furthermore, when Fidel Castro took power, Cuba had a flourishing rice industry on its way to make the country self-sufficient. Since 1962, rice rationing has persisted and even larger amounts of the grain have been imported annually to fulfill domestic demand.

The next quote is neither a promise nor a prediction. For Fidel Castro, it is a fact, a twisted number that makes one wonder how the Cuban people believed any of his statements. Here is the Aristotelian syllogism of November 22, 1991:[36] "Obviously, we are the country that produces the most food per capita in the world, because we feed four persons in the world for each citizen of this country. We export sugar calories for 40 million people. No country with so little land produces as much food per world inhabitant than Cuba. I say that to your satisfaction."

I do not believe that the statement made the listeners jump full of joy while chanting a peculiar Halloween riddle: "Trick **and** treat: take the food that we don't eat!" Making the necessary calculations to test the veracity of the claim would be a waste of time. First, Castro does not provide the needed assumptions. Second, in a country suffering a food crisis for the last 50 years, it is somewhat ironic to tell the people that they are feeding a good part of the world with the sugar calories they export —which, by the way, are substantially lower today than in 1991 when he made that statement. Therefore, Castro should deduct a large number of beneficiaries.

---

33 http://faostat.fao.org/site/339/default.aspx. It is the same reported by Cuba in its Statistical yearbook at http://www.one.cu/aec2011/esp/09_tabla_cuadro.htm.

34 http://faostat.fao.org/site/339/default.aspx.

35 http://geography.about.com/od/obtainpopulationdata/a/uspopulation.htm

36 http://www.cuba.cu/gobierno/discursos/1991/esp/f221191e.html.

Feeding the People

Signs of food scarcity were beginning to show less than two years after the triumph of the revolution in 1959, when the stocks in warehouses started declining and production was not enough to replace the quantities withdrawn. The population began to become alarmed and to show their discontent. The leadership faced a great challenge and needed to act quickly! Castro then came up with the idea of holding the "First National Production Assembly", in Havana's Chaplin Theatre at the end of August 1961. When one compares the promises and predictions of the parade of speakers shown life on national television, it is obvious that the spectacle was an orchestrated event, which culminated with a speaker sounding like a pathological liar. Fidel Castro assured the Cuban people that:[37] 1) by the month of December 1961 the entire supply shortage of poultry for the capital of the republic will be solved, and by February in all national markets; 2) starting January 1962, *vianda*[38] production will surpass the needs of the domestic market; 3) in June 1962, fish production will be sufficient to satisfy consumer needs; and 4) the current restrictions on fat distribution will end on January 1, 1963.

That they were all lies is not difficult to prove. First, there is no explanation on the mechanism to address the supply of poultry in four months for the capital and in six months for the entire country. Second, not even a miracle would lead to an oversupply of *viandas* in five months! Was Castro aware of the length of production cycles? Third, a prediction of ten months to fulfill the demand for fish appears more conservative. I assume that it took into account the time necessary to build up the Cuban fishing fleet, to catch the fish, and to establish the marketing channels. Perhaps, they were counting on the millions of trouts predicted earlier. Lastly, how did they estimate that it would take 18 months to eliminate the rationing of fat?

---

37 http://www.cuba.cu/gobierno/discursos/1961/esp/f280861e.html.

38 The term *vianda* includes *yucca* (cassava), *boniato* (sweet potato), *malanga* (taro), *calabaza* (pumpkin), and *ñame* (yam); sometimes it also includes *plátano* (plantain) and *papa* (potato).

The bottom line is that, more than 50 years later, all products listed above are still under the rationing system or sold in dollar stores, beyond the purchasing power of most Cubans.

The promises and predictions concerning food supplies continued. On January 2, 1965, Castro revealed expected production and consumption figures for eggs:[39] "We can say that, starting in the month of January [1965], 60 million eggs will be consumed monthly... We will have a consumption somewhat greater than 400% from January 1964 to January 1965. The 4 million layers needed to meet this plan are already laying."

Fidel Castro not only knew in advance population demand, but the month in which the layers would be producing eggs. At the beginning of the rationing system in 1962, each person could purchase two eggs per month, increasing later to between 15 and 24; later there were no quantity restrictions.[40] In July 2012, eggs had returned to the ration book at a rate of five per person per month at the subsidized price of 0.15 cents of a Cuban Peso (CUP). The additional five sold at 0.90 cents disappeared.[41] During the scarcity generated by the Spanish Civil War, Ramón Gómez de la Serna would come to the defense of the hens with his famous saying: "The hens are fed up of reporting in police stations that people are stealing their eggs. "[42]

---

39 http://www.cuba.cu/gobierno/discursos/1965/esp/f020165e.html.

40 Álvarez (2004a: 135).

41 http://www.havanatimes.org/?p=95726

42 From the monologue "El orador" of 1928. http://www.rtve.es/alacarta/videos/el-orador-o-la-mano/orador-mano-protagonizado-ramon-gomez-serna/1570987/.

Despite the failures described above, the population —still under ration-ing—was surprised in mid-2014 with the following announcement:

> Havana, May 22, 2014 (AIN) For his dedication and vigilance to boost the poultry industry in Cuba, the Commander in Chief Fidel Castro Ruz was awarded today the Distinction "50 years producing for the people."
>
> This special award was presented by Emiliano López Díaz, direc-tor of the National Poultry Combine (CAN) Gustavo Rodríguez, to the Minister of Agriculture, during the main event celebrating the half century of CAN's foundation.
>
> The award expresses the gratitude, pride and feelings of all poul-try workers of the country.

As is usually the case in times of scarcity, a parallel market developed to meet the needs at higher prices. Cuba was no exception. Fidel Castro did not like it and predicted its disappearance on January 21, 1965 at the time that he made the startling announcement that Cubans would be among the world's best-fed people in less than five years:[43] "That black market should be disappearing... In 1965 *viandas* will also disappear from the ration booklet. I have to tell the good news... By the year 1970, we will be, possibly, one of the best-fed people in the world, but we cannot consume only one thing: meat ... because meat is a commodity for which there is a tremendous demand on the world market. We have to have a balanced diet."

As demonstrated several times, the rationing system persists. According to press reports, corruption is rampant, as workers and managers steal from state stores and warehouses for consumption or black market sales.

---

43 http://www.cuba.cu/gobierno/discursos/1965/esp/f210165e.html.

Despite the long lines and waiting periods of sometimes several hours, the predictions of abundant supplies continued. On July 17, 1968, Fidel discussed a wide range of products and total agricultural output[44] He predicted that, in 1970, only eleven years after the triumph of the revolution, Cuba's total agricultural output may have increased by 100%. Yet, from that year on, it will still grow at a very significant rate, because starting that year there will actually be increases in production of a number of other commodities like citrus, coffee and milk, which should increase about 4 million liters daily per year. Another Patty the Milkmaid counting followed: "… meaning that if we get four in 1970, we will achieve eight in 1971, twelve in 1972, growing at that rate until reaching the production of thirty million liters of milk per day in 1975!" This time the Milkmaid would need a trailer to carry her pails of milk to market. The image of the ration booklet is a reminder of the falsehood of those statements.

On July 14, 1969, it was rice's turn again: "we have said on previous occasions that in 1971 we would be self-sufficient in rice, but we can say something more: in 1971 we will have large surpluses of rice for export." [45]

---

44 http://www.cuba.cu/gobierno/discursos/1968/esp/f170768e.html.

45 http://www.cuba.cu/gobierno/discursos/1969/esp/f140769e.html.

FAOSTAT reports that Cuba did not export any rice in 1971.[46] In fact, Cuba has been an importer of rice since the beginning of the revolution. Recently, annual rice imports have been around 500,000 metric tons of milled rice.[47]

The final prediction of this section concerning the future abundance of food occurred on May 18, 1967, when Castro stated,[48] "The day will come when, as the result of the increases in production, money will have no value whatsoever." So untrue that Cuba today is struggling with three different currencies: the Cuban Peso (CUP), the Convertible Peso (CUC) and the US dollar.

The Geneticist

Fidel Castro had many dreams. One of them was the development of a Cuban race of livestock that would surpass all others in milk and meat production. In simple words, he wanted to create a Cuban cow. Chapter 7 discusses his genetic revolution. Despite his efforts to play that role, he was not a geneticist. On February 19, 1965, he described the crosses to make in order to arrive at his goal.[49] In the future, instead of having Zebu cattle, Cuba's cattle will be three quarters Holstein, one-fourth Zebu; or three-fourths Brown Swiss; or five- or seven-eighths Brown Swiss and one-eighth Zebu. That would transform all that cattle into dairy cattle that will produce milk and meat from the use of genetics in solving that problem. Castro's vision included cattle that would be good milk producers, good producers of meat, and he counted those cows by the millions.

The fact remains that milk is still under the rationing system and beef is inexistent. Concerning the millions of cows, there were 0.83 heads of livestock per person in 1959, decreasing to 0.52 in 1975-79 and to 0.4 in 1986-89 (see chapter 4). According to Cuba's statistical yearbook, there were 4.1 million heads of cattle on December 31, 2011.[50] With a population of 11,247,925, that works out to 0.364 heads per capita.

---

46 http://faostat.fao.org/site/342/default.aspx.

47 http://en.wikipedia.org/wiki/Agriculture_in_Cuba#Rice.

48 http://www.cuba.cu/gobierno/discursos/1967/esp/f180567e.html.

49 http://www.cuba.cu/gobierno/discursos/1965/esp/f190265e.html.

50 http://www.one.cu/aec2011/esp/09_tabla_cuadro.htm.

Castro's scientific mind led him to conduct numerous experiments. The following joke dated January 30, 1969, describes a *sui generis* research: Red color makes the cows more resistant to Cuba's hot climate. For that reason, he started gathering all red ones to develop red Holstein with all their features except their color. The literature reports that, since the glands that determine the cow's dairy behavior are in the head, it would suffice to change the climate in the head of the animal. That theory was undergoing testing at "Niña Bonita Dos" where, instead of using air conditioning in the entire facility, only the heads of the cows receive it in a small room. Just at the outset of the trial, Castro estimated that the practice would translate into using 25% of the previous energy consumption of the whole facility.[51] The interested reader can admire the hilarious and expensive photograph in several sites of the Internet.[52]

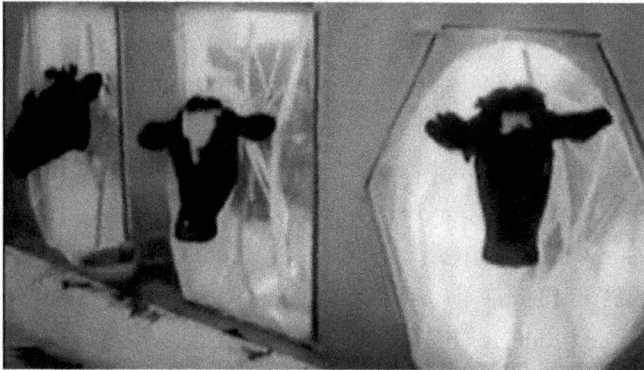

The apparent joke in fact has a scientific base. Since the early 1960s, animal researchers have been looking into the relationships between climatic conditions and dairy behavior.[53] Castro, however, departed from the findings by limiting the change of climate just to the heads —something that the specialists had not realized for saving energy.

---

51 http://www.cuba.cu/gobierno/discursos/1969/esp/f300169e.html.

52 See, for example, http://octavocercoen.blogspot.com/2009_11_01_archive.html;and also http://www.cubademocraciayvida.org/web/article.asp?artID=22841.

53 See, for example, the article entitled "The lactating cow in the various ecosystems: environmental effects on its productivity," by H.D. Johnson at http://www.fao.org/docrep/003/t0413e/t0413e02.htm.

The Sugar Industry

The promises and predictions related to the sugar industry cover a wide range of topics and degrees of impossibility. Let us start with one that shows his belief that Cuba is his farm: "I expect to obtain the equivalent of eight tons of sugar per acre in one year... I am certain that I will obtain those quantities."[54] The statements were made in the context of an imaginary competition with yields in Hawaii, which, needless to say, he lost.

Castro was aware of the importance of diversification within the sugar industry. On June 7, 1965, he described his conception of the Cuban sugar industry of the future. He dreamed with a modern industry that would include suchrochemistry, paper from bagasse, the mixing of bagasse pulp with wood pulp for export and the production not only of 10 million tons of sugar but another 4 million tons of honey that will make Cuba also a meat exporter.[55]

The truth is that, in the five sugar campaigns from 2005-06 to 2009-10, Cuba produced an average of 1.25 million metric tons of sugar per harvest,[56] similar to the levels obtained in 1894 and 1895.[57] The meat-exporting goal never materialized.

The next statement is of utmost importance because it reveals that Castro's promises and predictions were not the result of a false optimism or erroneous information he received. On December 20, 1969, in the midst of the 10-million-ton sugar harvest, when Fidel Castro already knew the truth that several specialists had been telling him for years, that it was impossible to achieve that goal, he lied to a graduating class of economists. Not only did he tell them how well the harvest was going but predicted crops of over 20 million tons of sugar with current technology. And also 24 or 25 million tons with the extra land assigned in the Prospective Plan. He got so fired up that ended his comments predicting: "Maybe, with future techniques, in 1980 one would have to put the potential at 27 or 28 [million tons]."[58]

---

54 Lockwood (1990: 88).

55 http://www.cuba.cu/gobierno/discursos/1965/esp/f070665e.html.

56 http://www.one.cu/aec2011/esp/11_tabla_cuadro.htm.

57 Thomas (1971: 1562).

58 http://www.cuba.cu/gobierno/discursos/1969/esp/f201269e.html.

Not only did he lie in relation to the current harvest, but also he dared to predict outputs of 27 or 28 million metric tons for 1980 and beyond. As already mentioned above, Cuba has been producing between 1 and 2 million metric tons in recent years.

A House for Every Family

Owning a home —or at least having a roof under our heads—is perhaps one of the most important goals of a family. At the triumph of the revolution, the national lottery system became the Savings and Housing Institute with the proceeds going to finance housing construction for the people. On February 16, 1959, Castro promised: "I can tell you that, with the passing of time, the Savings and Housing Institute will build all the houses the country needs."[59] All the houses the country needs —in rural and urban areas— was an overwhelming challenge. The contrast between that statement and today's reality could not have been more disappointing.

In the early 2000s, the housing deficit had grown to 1.6 million (for a population of 11.2 million), and 39% of the existing housing stock did not meet habitability standards.[60] The Savings and Housing Institute disappeared in March 1968.[61]

Paying or Defaulting?

The foreign debt was a hot topic during many years. Although Fidel Castro launched an international campaign (and even held meetings in Havana) to convince third-world countries not to pay the debt, he had promised the opposite on January 2, 1965: "In addition, we will not fail to pay any capitalist country... we will always pay every penny... we will end up not owing a single penny to anyone." [62]

---

59 http://www.cuba.cu/gobierno/discursos/1959/esp/c160259e.html.
60 Oficina Nacional de Estadísticas (ONE). *Anuario Estadístico de Cuba:* http://www.one.cu/
61 http://www.ecured.cu/index.php/Instituto_Nacional_de_Ahorro_y_Viviendas.
62 http://www.cuba.cu/gobierno/discursos/1965/esp/f020165e.html.

Cuba's external debt in December 31, 2012 was around US $ 22.36 billion.[63] Cuba also owed some US $ 25 billion to the former Soviet Union just partially forgiven, causing concern to the members of the Paris Club.[64] (See chapter 12). Lack of fresh credit is due to Cuba's inability (and unwillingness) to pay its bills. Some people in Cuba say that defaulting on its debts is Cuba's major source of foreign exchange.

Enlarging Cuba

For Fidel Castro, perhaps Cuba was too small an island for the plans he had. Therefore, he decided to expand it. As an archipelago, small and not-so-small keys surround the main island. The largest one is the former Isle of Pines (later renamed Isle of Youth). The distance that separates it from the mainland is about 75 miles (120 km).[65] On August 12, 1967, Castro announced that the government was studying the geology of the region between the Isle of Pines and the province of Havana, considering the possibility of building levees in those shallow waters to dissect the entire region.[66]

A visual inspection of the map is more meaningful than a written explanation and I invite the reader to consider Cuba's resources to carry out a project of such magnitude.

---

63 http://www.indexmundi.com/cuba/debt_external.html.

64 http://www.reuters.com/article/2013/03/14/cuba-debt-russia-idUSL1N0C592Z20130314.

65 http://www.cubacasas.net/cities/nueva_gerona/

66 http://www.cuba.cu/gobierno/discursos/1967/esp/f120867e.html.

José Álvarez, Ph.D.

A Final Comment

It is extremely difficult to abstain from using sarcasm while making comments after each of Castro's promises and predictions. Montaner[67] wonders if they were said with the intention to delude the people or were just the result of ignorance. He bets for the second, but he does it with hesitation. He states that there is nothing more dangerous than a euphoric ignorant, and that Castro and his inner circle were textbook examples of that group. I disagree. I believe that it was ignorance to some extent, but there was the intention to deceive, some degree of insanity and, above all, a well-prepared plan to stay in power for as long as he could.

The evidence is overwhelming. Fidel Castro was constantly moving the goalposts further away. Dates for the fulfillment of production targets changed to later dates, to an ever-increasing distant horizon difficult to visualize. The remaining pages show statements and actions that appear to have come from a Don Quixote suffering from a severe degree of delusion, but the firm goal of remaining in power until the last day of his life. The following chapter on leadership theory provides some necessary background to understand how he did it.

---

67 (1994: 187).

Chapter 2

LEADERSHIP THEORY AND CASTRO'S DECISION MAKING

De Minimis Non Curat Praetor.
[The chief does not concern himself with trifles].[1]

*I*n Gabriel García Márquez's *The general in his labyrinth*, the main character, despite past glories, is trying to escape from South America to exile in Europe. The author describes a prematurely aged Simón Bolívar who is physically ill and mentally exhausted.

When I read that book in 1990, Castro was beginning to face the greatest challenge of his 32-year old regime that began with the fall of the Berlin Wall and led to the dissolution of the Soviet Union. He had turned 64 a few weeks earlier and was in excellent health.

Although not the content, at least the title seems to fit the theme of this book. The previous chapter provides a few episodes of Castro's labyrinth. An explanation for his behavior is lacking. As the Colombian writer did with his Bolivar, it is necessary to depart from the traditional heroic portrait of Castro to unveil the rosary of failures generated by the projects he championed during almost five decades. Can leadership theory be a useful tool to do so? Following

---

1 The quote, in Latin and English appears in http://en.wikipedia.org/wiki/De_minimis. Webster defines "praetor" as a magistrate in ancient Rome, translated here as "chief". Dumont (1970: 54) describes that, while arguing with Castro about the nature and scope of the communal farms, Castro handed him a sketch he had drawn specifying the location of the cowshed, its grazing lands, the pigsty, and the fields to grow crops.

the Spanish philosopher Ortega y Gasset ("I am I and my circumstance"), it is necessary not only to analyze the man and his leadership traits but also his life environment, especially his early upbringing in Birán –where his parents' farm was located— that appears to have marked him for the rest of his life. I have found several events during Castro's life in Birán that appear to have led him on the road to become the supreme pontiff of Cuba's agricultural sector.

Some General Concepts

This chapter focuses on Fidel Castro's personality traits, based on three related concepts: charisma, narcissism and *caudillismo* (autocratic government).

According to the Spanish Royal Academy (RAE),[2] a *"caudillo"* is a "man that as head, guides and commands people during war" or a "man who leads a syndicate, community or body". From the analysis to follow, it becomes clear that Fidel Castro is a *caudillo* and his administration falls under the category of an autocratic government.

Fidel Castro, however, is a peculiar *caudillo*. Most people tend to associate Spain's Generalissimo Francisco Franco with the word *"caudillo"*. A Cuban-American[3] scholar studied parallels and contrasts between Franco and Castro to conclude that the two famous caudillos show more contrasts than similarities.[4] The same author[5] delved into the possibility of Castro being a Machiavellian prince, concluding: "Castro, although matching the Machiavellian prince in most respects, is fundamentally different from him. Machiavelli's prince is not a tyrant, as the ancients understood the term. Fidel Castro is". One may ask what type of tyrant is Castro?

Two researchers[6] place Castro's regime among the hybrid dictatorships, defined as "those that blend qualities of personalist, single-party and military dictatorships". They corroborate the thesis of this book by stating, "Castro

---

2 http://www.rae.es/rae.html.

3 Cuzán (2004).

4 See Sondrol (1991) for a comparison with Paraguay's Stroessner.

5 Cuzán (1999: 190).

6 Ezrow and Frants (2011:22, 266-267).

was in charge of all major policy decisions… Like a personalist dictator, Castro played a central role in the making of policy. Decision-making in Cuba inevitably required Castro's input… Castro's charismatic personalist and revolutionary discourse also enhanced his rule". In no other area of his administration –with the exception of education and relations with the United States—was his charismatic personality more relevant than in agriculture.

Very few people would deny that Castro possesses charisma.[7] Kling[8] states that he "easily qualifies as a charismatic leader. His political style is colorful, extreme, flamboyant, and theatrical. He disdains conventions and routine procedures and conspicuously departs from organizational norms of behavior and appearance".

To understand the personal meaning of charismatic leaders, according to Hermans,[9] valuation theory provides a useful framework. This theory proposes two basic motives that drive an individual's behavior: self-glorification and self-transcendence. The former influences one's meaning of life experience by protection, maintaining and aggrandizing one's self-esteem. It is also consistent with self aggrandizing/narcissistic orientations of destructive charismatic leaders.[10]

Sosik believes that personality traits help define the personal meaning of charismatic leaders. A leader may be a socialized charismatic leader who possesses an egalitarian, self-transcendent, and empowering personality, or a personalized charismatic leader who possesses a dominant, Machiavellian and narcissistic personality.[11]

What is narcissism? According to Rosenthal and Pittinsky, it is:[12] "A personality trait encompassing grandiosity, arrogance, self-absorption, entitlement, fragile self-esteem, and hostility, is an attribute of many powerful leaders. Narcissist leaders have grandiose belief systems and leadership styles, and are

---

7 Fagen (1965) contains a very good treatment of this topic.

8 (1962: 45-46).

9 1998, as it appears in John J. Sosik (2000).

10 Padilla et al (2007) use Fidel Castro's destructive leadership to illustrate the dynamics of their framework.

11 As defined by House and Howell (1992). See also Bream (2004).

12 (2006: 617).

generally motivated by their needs for power and admiration rather than empathetic concern for the constituents and institutions they lead."

The testimony of a former high-ranking officer of Cuba's intelligence apparatus, who defected to the United States, seems to corroborate how that definition fits Castro while describing him as he delivered a speech to Cuban troops in Angola:[13]

> He was euphoric, glorying in what he had accomplished in Angola and elsewhere in Africa and other Cold War conflict zones. The speech was all about his triumphs, his valor, his audacity, and his exceptional leadership qualities. He said almost nothing about the contributions of the uniformed men arrayed before him or the sacrifices of the many Cuban dead... Fidel compared himself to the Nazi propaganda chieftain Joseph Goebbels: "Castro said he could lead the multitudes better than Goebbels. That is how he said it... how to guide people to do what you want them to do." It was fidelista hubris in the most heinous extreme.

At this point, I want to insert an important characteristic of Castro's personality that may very well approach the physiological area: He apparently believes he has the power of transfiguration. Yes, like Jesus in Mount Tabor. I have not forgotten listening to a conference by the late Enrique Baloyra referring to Castro's reinventing himself according to the circumstances. While introducing guerrilla warfare in Latin America he would pretend to have become Caupolicán, the Araucanian chief and a leader of the Indian resistance to the Spanish invaders of Chile. A few months later, his will would transform him into Scipio the African, turned against the imperial powers sending invasions to "liberate" countries on the continent.

The American Psychiatric Association (APA)[14] has concluded that a diagnosis of narcissist personality must include at least five of the following nine attributes: 1) Grandiose sense of self-importance. 2) Preoccupation with fantasies of unlimited success or power. 3) Belief in "special" or unique status (including

---

13 Florentino Aspillaga shared his experience with Brian Latell (2012: 5).
14 APA (2000: 717).

fixation on associating with high-status people or institutions). 4) Requirement for excessive admiration. 5) Unreasonable sense and expectations of entitlement. 6) Interpersonal exploitativeness. 7) Lack of empathy. 8) Envy. 9) Arrogant behavior or attitudes.

Are charisma and narcissism related? Galvin et al.[15] tested a model that portrays the roles of socialized vision and visionary boldness as mediators in the relationship between narcissism and charisma. Their findings suggest that narcissism is positively related to vision boldness and negatively related to socialized visions. In turn, both aspects of vision are positively associated with attributions of charisma.

The following pages will show that Fidel Castro has more than the minimum traits required by the APA for a passing narcissist grade.[16]

Castro's Personality Traits

Most of the nine aforementioned attributes manifest themselves in Fidel Castro's behavior and actions when dealing with the agricultural sector:

- Posturing as a man of science (# 9: arrogant behavior or attitudes).
- Prevalence of politics over science (# 5: Unreasonable sense and expectations of entitlement).
- Impromptu decisions with no prior studies (# 2: Preoccupation with fantasies of unlimited success or power; # 9: arrogant behavior or attitudes).
- Advice is unheeded and criticism forbidden (# 1: grandiose sense of self-importance; # 9: arrogant behavior or attitudes).
- An authoritarian and proprietor's attitude (# 7: lack of empathy; # 8: envy).
- Assuming the leadership role of his own opposition (# 5: Unreasonable sense and expectations of entitlement; # 9: arrogant behavior or attitudes).

Posturing as a Man of Science

In a 1969 speech, Castro stated that he did not consider his interventions in the agricultural sector to be a fault. His responsibilities to the people, he reasoned,

---

15 Galvin, Waldman and Balthazard (2010).
16 Marques (2007) contains a list of Fidel Castro's most listed positive and negative qualities.

forced him "to study and learn a little to try to find solutions, mainly because of Cuba's scarcity of scientists and technicians".[17] Then he specified that he was not newcomer to genetics. Forced by the circumstances, he had to search for solutions and was always open to reasonable and clear ideas. "We do not pretend to be scientists. That would be absurd... We aim at acquiring a minimum of knowledge to be able to evaluate the information given to us."

The repetition of his denial of being a scientist, while claiming the right to act like one due to necessity, reveals the opposite belief: "Fortunately, I do not presume being either a speaker or a scientist.[18] What are the risks I will be running if I start talking about scientific matters?[19] Since the very first moment, we were aware of the importance of science. I believe we know some today; it is not enough... [However] the visitors should not imagine that our scientific effort has been exempt of errors, stumbles and failures."[20]

The truth of the matter is that Fidel Castro always believed he was a scientist, and behaved accordingly. When he was interested in a topic, his long speeches intended to show the audience that he knew best.[21] The following variety of topics and circumstances are just a few examples to illustrate that point:[22]

- Domestic sugar policy and agricultural development, at the assembly of sugarcane producers held on April 4, 1959.
- Dynamics of pastures, at the opening ceremony of a series of conferences on "Influences of soils on animals through plants", by professor Andre Voisin,

---

17 Castro (1990: 117-118).

18 Speech at the Academy of Science's meeting of the Cuba's Speleological Society on January 15, 1960 (http://www.cuba.cu/gobierno/discursos/1960/esp/f150160e.html).

19 http://www.cuba.cu/gobierno/discursos/1964/esp/f081264e.html.

20 Speech at the XXX anniversary of the Cuban Academy of Sciences, February 20, 1992 (http://www.cuba.cu/gobierno/discursos/1992/esp/f200292e.html).

21 People who have been close to Castro testify to his extraordinary memory, which he has used since his early years. For example, Szulc (1986) refers to his "computer-like memory" (p. 39), "prodigious memory" (pp. 79, 161, 577), "selective memory" (p. 107), "phenomenal memory" (p. 115), "stunning memory" (p. 120), "fabulous memory" (p. 177), "willpower and superb memory" (p. 193), "monumental memory" (p. 297), and "flexible memory" (p. 503).

22 These examples appear in the official website of Castro's speeches at http://www.cuba.cu/gobierno/discursos.

Doctor Honoris Causa of the Veterinary School of Bonn and member of France's Academy of Sciences, on December 8, 1964.

- Genetics for cattle improvement, at the Niña Bonita genetic experimental plan, on January 30, 1969; at the first congress of the Institute of Animal Science, held on May 13, 1969; and at the 25th anniversary of the establishment of Los Naranjos genetic enterprise on May 26, 1989.

If the previous examples were not enough, the following incident will shed more light about this aspect of his personality. Obsessed as he was with the development of a "tropical cow" for his country, he would not allow anyone to contradict his knowledge of genetics. In the first congress of the Institute of Animal Science on May 13, 1969, a paper was presented by Dr. T.R. Preston[23] and Dr. H.B. Willis,[24] international animal nutritionist experts working at Cuba's Animal Science Institute (ICA). The scientists expressed their doubts about the massive crossings of dairy cattle with Zebu, with the resulting hybrid called F-1 (See diagram in chapter 7).

Fidel Castro replied immediately. He embarked in a long speech about previous experimental results, with detailed analyses of data, and arguments intended to show him right and the foreign scientists wrong.[25] Then, he added: "That [paper] was presented here, although it was called "internal". Because I would not dare to present something "internal", something that does not have minimum validity. It is not to present for the sake of presenting. However, this thesis was presented by a member of the Institute and endorsed by the principal geneticist of the institution and its director."

---

23 Dr. T.R. Preston was born in England and obtained his P.D. at Newcastle University in 1955. He went to Cuba at the beginning of the revolution, helped design, and later directed the Institute of Animal Science from 1965 to 1971. He is a famous international consultant of animal nutrition. In 1976, he received the Sir John Hammond Award from the British Society of Animal Science.

24 Dr. H.B. Willis, an American animal scientist, worked with Dr. Preston in the first years of the revolution in the Institute of Animal Science. He worked on genetics and nutrition. He co-authored with Dr. Preston a paper entitled "The development of research programs to ensure continuity in the face of political change" *Panel on Post Graduate Education and Associated Research for the Support of Livestock Development in Latin America.* Turrialba, Costa Rica, August 25-29, 1969.

25 Http://www.cuba.cu/gobierno/discursos/1969/esp/f130569e.html. A similar incident took place at another congress. A European scientist was presenting a paper advocating cereals, while Castro was defending the idea of pasture and sugarcane (http://lanic.utexas.edu).

That was not enough for Castro. He then proceeded to speak as an official refereed of the paper: "Is there proof for their hypothesis? No, there is not. Is there research to support it? Yes, this can be investigated and proven: the nature of this paper, its low quality and the superficiality of the research, the errors inherent in the paper, the lack of orientation in this paper to the ranchers of this country and to those who work in cattle production, to those who already own half-million F-1 cows."

Castro then reveals the reason for the temper tantrum:

> Now, is this about us getting mad because an investigation shows negative results? No. What really makes us mad is that a paper contradicts reality, leading to a false conclusion... Honestly, without question, subjective factors influenced the research. The data are here.

The absurdity of the situation did not end there. Dr. Willis also presented a paper concluding that the Zebu's capacity to resist heat and other elements was the result of its productive incapacity. "And, with all respect," Castro stated, "we disagree with that point of view". Then he devoted a considerable amount of time to prove again that he was right and Dr. Willis was wrong.

His experiments in area of animal nutrition continued. During his closing speech of the National Technical Encounter about Hay, Silage and Intensive Grazing, held on July 20, 1963, Castro had posed as a research scientist, this time in the area of poultry nutrition:[26] He said he had been experimenting with some hens that graze and lay eggs. Results had shown that, after three months, the hens that had two ounces of feed and grazed in pastures began to produce more than those eating four ounces of feed alone. He finished the description with an unhidden pride: "I want you to know that, and I can give accurate information because I did that experiment personally."

Two years earlier, Castro had explained another experiment he had performed. He did it in his speech at the commencement ceremony for 200 peasants receiving a diploma as artificial inseminators on December 12, 1961. He was

---

26 http://www.cuba.cu/gobierno/discursos/1963/esp/f200763e.html.

recommending the establishment of small research groups in each state farm; Castro had recently formed one such group himself with the members of his security detail. The objective of their first experiment was to plant three crops (tigernut, kidney beans and sago, with seeds from Spain) next to each other and let them grow until the pigs were brought to that lot to eat. The crops were then mowed and let regrow. His men agreed and were so enthusiastic that worked with him close to midnight and started planting in the backyard of a nearby house. He was sure that "the future of swine rising"[27] depended on his experiment.[28]

Fidel Castro had already forgotten his humble confession of 1964, during his inaugural speech of André Voisin's cycle of conferences about the dynamics of grazing: "I, as a politician, run risks if I start talking about scientific issues. Surely, a scientist has fewer chances of being wrong when making a political judgment than a politician when he makes a scientific judgment"[29] Dumont[30] reveals that Fidel's experiments are conducted on the best soils and with all the required resources. "He is the one who knows everything and the peasants admire him. Castro believes himself to be the most capable person to perform the synthesis of science and common sense."

Despite Castro's alleged scientific mind, many decisions depended more on what the politics of the moment dictate rather than on scientific results.

Prevalence of Politics over Science

During his long interview with Lee Lockwood, Castro justified his scientific endeavors in the following manner: "... technicians often have conflicting ideas and do not analyze production problems from a political point of view. Therefore, we must know at least enough [about science] to be able to evaluate their opinions. "[31] Castro was willing to make a decision involving a quick

---

27 I have not included the famous "Swine plan" (Plan porcino) because it is very similar to the rest of the livestock efforts.

28 http://www.cuba.cu/gobierno/discursos/1961/esp/f121261e.html.

29 Speech of 8 December 1964: http://www.cuba.cu/gobierno/discursos/1964/esp/f081264e.html.

30 (1971: 169).

31 Lockwood (1990: 87).

political gain rather than wait to obtain a huge economic gain in the medium- or long-term. He confessed not knowing "how to distinguish between science and politics except that science and politics are both an art".[32] In a May 13, 1969 speech[33] he had referred to statements made like "the political part ends and science starts... and it is fair that if we place science in its place and we praise and support it, there can't be distinctions between science and politics". There is no need to point out to the contradiction!

A similar problem originated during the celebration of the First Congress of the Animal Science Institute, on May 13, 1969, when Dr. Preston also hinted that political issues had been an obstacle to choosing the proper fodder in Cuba. In his speech, Castro was swift in his response.[34] He expressed doubts about what country Dr. Preston was referring to, because in Cuba there were neither social nor political obstacles to develop cattle feeds based on corn. But it needed to be proven first.

Two Cuban scientists refer to 1959-1974 as a "period of directed science promotion", characterized by a series of decision-making measures aimed at establishing and equipping research institutions, "but under the higher orientation of the Revolutionary Government toward the solution of crucial problems of socio-economic development".[35] That is, the prevalence of politics over science.

Two foreign economists working in Cuba at that time provide further proof. Gutelman[36] realized the obvious political nature of the great majority of the economic and technical decisions made by the revolution. Chonchol[37] found the danger of subordinating economic and social aspects to considerations of a political nature more difficult than training sugarcane farmers for a diversified agriculture.

I have selected, as final testimony for this section, the words that Dr. Willis told Reckord:[38] "Scientific policies could be carried out across the board. No

---

32 Castro (1990: 116).

33 Speech at the first congress of the Institute of Animal Science, May 13, 1969. (http://www.cuba.cu/gobierno/discursos/1969/espf130569e.html).

34 http://www.cuba.cu/gobierno/discursos/1969/esp/f130569e.html.

35 Sáenz and Capote (1989: 88-89).

36 (1967: 75).

37 (1963: 128).

38 (1971: 149-150).

private interests or stubborn ancient customs to interfere. But instead politics interfered; Fidel was a politician dabbling in science. This was fatal. Politics and science didn't mix."

Impromptu Decisions with No Prior Studies

One of the central features of Castro's decision-making were the sudden impulses leading to the immediate implementation of projects that, if subject to previous analyses or feasibility studies, would show their unfeasibility. Dumont[39] was perhaps the first foreign expert to identify Castro's audacity for undertaking projects along with his disdain for feasibility studies:[40] "Many of those projects had some value, and their failures originate in the audacity of the "maximum leader", the great chief, in launching them too fast and in a very large scale, without performing exhaustive preliminary studies. Fidel believes he knows everything in several domains much better than the rest. His pride is his worst enemy."[41]

Even Aranda, an apologetic foreign advisor during the 1960s,[42] had to recognize that massive works to expand an area planted to traditional crops or to introduce new ones, or to develop systems of intensive livestock management were reduced or eliminated. One of the reasons was "the lack of exhaustive and detailed studies that could have signaled forthcoming difficulties".[43] In the case

---

39   René Dumont, French agronomist and socialist militant, travelled to Cuba invited twice invited by Fidel Castro in 1960, and once by Carlos Rafael Rodríguez in 1963, as an agricultural expert. He returned in 1969 as Castro's personal guest. His reports are full of constructive criticisms that were never accepted and of ignored recommendations.

40   Roca (1994: 100) lists a series of projects for which he found no evidence of prior technical and economic evaluations: micro jet irrigation systems, field drainage for sugarcane, leveling technique for rice, Voisin's rational grazing system, sheep raising in special soils with zeolite, a national irrigation system with massive locks and canals, and animal-feed based on sugar byproducts.

41   Dumont (1971: 72).

42   In the Introduction to his book, Aranda (1975) recognizes the existence of "deficiencies". He adds that they are widely discussed in the press and official speeches. For that reason, his view of not emphasizing them "does not correspond to a preconceived idea to embellish reality by abstracting from defects, but the author's criterion that what characterize Cuban agricultural development are not the defects but the achievements" (p. 4).

43   Aranda (1975: 42-43).

of the sugarcane field drainage method (*drenaje parcelario*), the advice of local technicians was not followed.[44]

Advice is Unheeded and Criticism Forbidden

As predicted by leadership theory, field drainage was not the only case where advice was unheeded. Mitchell and Rossmoore[45] have studied the issue, concluding that leaders must replace their internal programming that rejects good advice and should examine or question their own thinking. Perhaps that is a good explanation for Castro's decision-making behavior.

Castro always paid attention only to the recommendations he liked. Once he made a decision, criticism was out of the question. Fidel Castro did not admit dissent from his view and seldom followed the advice provided by foreign advisors and local scientists when their opinions contradicted his.[46] Those traits surfaced several times during his relationship with Dumont:[47] "Fidel Castro was a magnificent fighter, and he is a born educator, but he continues to underestimate technical and economic difficulties. He believes himself to be more capable than other people of finding the best solutions, and always reasons like a guerrilla. His economic errors have cost Cuba dearly... Fidel should acquire a little of the humility of men who are truly great."[48]

Too often, you hear in Cuba: "You're right, but Fidel doesn't agree". He seems to be a stubborn man, and his opinion remains gospel regardless of the cost.[49]

The French agronomist added an interesting note about another of Castro's strategies when facing criticism from foreign visitors: "All the foreign friends

---

44 Zumaquero Posada, et al. (1991: 141).

45 (2001: 79-105).

46 There are numerous examples of both. Hagelberg and Álvarez (2006) have several instances.

47 Dumont (1970: 214-215).

48 When Dumont told Castro the statistics given to him by two Cuban doctors on the number of physicians who had left Cuba in the early years of the revolution, "Fidel Castro... contradicted me with his usual impetus: "More than half left". He knows everything, better than his collaborators" (1971: 72n15).

49 (1970: 154n18).

who visit us have nothing but compliments for us, whereas all you ever seem to do is criticize. Why do you criticize us?"[50]

Another example of this type of behavior became obvious during the first congress of the Animal Science Institute of May 13, 1969, already mentioned. At the opening ceremony, Dr. T.R. Preston had expressed his disagreement with the organization of the event. During his speech at the closing ceremony, Castro attacked Dr. Preston.[51] During the inauguration, Castro expressed, Dr. Preston complained about the Congress not being what it was supposed to be and expressed his disagreement, pointing out that the prior discussion of that issue allowed him to exercise the same right to explain what really happened. He said that another comrade referred to "misunderstandings", "stumbling blocks to science" and who knows how many other things. Then, he asked: "What is that?" He reasoned that, since that had happened at the inauguration [when Castro was absent], there was a need to do so at the closing also. There was more. Other institutions were offended and hurt. And Castro continued: "do you need to say that in this country's first congress —as if we were some sort of *siboneyes*[52], or something like that, a backward country— the President of the session —who was the President of the Academy of Sciences— was reading a newspaper... What was the need to open those wounds? On top of that, there was the expression that Cubans were going to learn how to behave in an international Congress... Unfortunately, these things happened. We ought to address the issue and provide an answer."

The 10-million ton sugar campaign is a good example of his reluctance to listen to advice from both foreign and domestic specialists (see chapter 7). In the domestic bureaucracy, they included, among others, Herrera[53] --sugar specialist and regular contributor in the ideological journal *Cuba Socialista*—who wrote about the problems that the agricultural sector would face, sugar minister

---

50 Dumont (1970: 41).

51 http://www.cuba.cu/gobierno/discursos/1969/esp/f130569e.html.

52 There is the belief that *siboneyes* were the first inhabitants of what later would be known as Cuba.

53 (1965).

Borrego Díaz,[54] who discussed problems related to the industrial sector, and Regalado —old revolutionary and member of ANAP's National Directorate--,[55] who voiced his worries about small sugarcane farmers. It is important to point out that these people stated publicly their disagreement with the official campaign as early as 1965, at the beginning of the Prospective Plan. For that, and for warning about the negative impacts that such plan would have on the rest of the economy, Orlando Borrego Díaz lost his position as minister of sugar in 1968, ironically when it had become obvious to many others that he had been right. Foreign advisors who shared the opinion of the domestic technicians included, among others, Dumont,[56] Gutelman,[57] and Aranda.[58]

In early 1964, Dumont had cautioned Castro that the 10-million ton goal was out of reach before 1975, if then, "and the 1968 harvest will perhaps not be even six million tons or a return to what it was in 1958".[59]

Michel Gutelman, a French economist who worked in Cuba in the early years of the revolution, based his opinion on installed industrial capacity. He argued that a $150 million investment in industry would increase production from seven to eight and a half million tons. To jump from seven to 10 million tons, the investment required would run around one billion dollars. He would rather invest that amount in other sectors that would substitute imported goods and produce new products for export, with productivity greater than in the sugar sector.[60]

In an ex-post scenario, Sergio Aranda reasoned that, "to produce 10 million tons of sugar, average national yields from now [1967] to 1970 would have to increase by approximately 40%" which he considered a titanic effort.[61] Expert

---

54 (1965).
55 (1965).
56 (1970).
57 (1967).
58 (1975).
59 Dumont (1970: 214).
60 Gutelman (1967: 184).
61 Aranda (1975: 68).

after expert repeated the advice (backed up by numbers) but to no avail. Fidel Castro had already set the goal: 10 million tons.

If the reader wonders about the origin of the 10-million ton target, not a single soul in Cuba had any doubt, but no proof. It was not until 2010 that the confirmation came. In recent years, interested Cubans attend an event called "Last Thursday Forum", held at the Cinema Institute, where a panel of experts,[62] with public participation, discusses relevant topics. On July 29, 2010, the topic was the 10-million ton campaign.

Selma Díaz, a member of the panel, revealed that she had been part the groups analyzing industrial capacity in the mid-1960s. She candidly expressed: "When that commission met with our commander-in-chief, they told him that it was only possible to produce eight and a half million tons. He said that it should be nine, and at the next meeting, he increased the figure to 10."

Despite the previous testimonies, and after recognizing publicly his responsibility in the failure, Castro blamed the planning apparatus and the Ministry of Sugar (MINAZ), dismissing the Minister, engineer Francisco Padrón, who had replaced Borrego, with the following insulting remarks that should have been aimed at Castro himself:

> Now, the "technocrats," the "smart ones," the "wise ones," the "super scientists," knew what had to be done in order to produce 10 million [tons]. But it was proven, first that they really did not know what had to be done and, second, that they exploited the rest of the economy by receiving large amounts of resources.[63]

The issue, however, was not "what had to be done" because everyone knew that it was increasing industrial capacity. Castro implied that the technocrats kept the secret to make the campaign fail. They had told him many times. To blame others for the diversion of the country's resources to the sugarcane harvest is

---

62 This panel was composed by Selma Díaz, Julio Díaz Vázquez and Juan Valdés Paz, well known professionals who had participated in the 1970 campaign. This information appears in "Ten million and forty years later", by Yusimi Rodríguez, appearing in *Havana Times* on August 16, 2010 at http://www.havanatimes.org/?p=27804.

63 Speech at the CTC's provincial plenary held at the CTC theatre, 3 of September 1970: http://www.cuba.cu/gobierno/discursos/1970/esp/f030970e.html.

a malicious accusation when everybody knows that Fidel Castro was the only person in Cuba who had the power to do that.

An Authoritarian and Proprietor's Attitude

Numerous examples show these personality traits.[64] As stated above, people tell you in Cuba that you are right, "but Fidel doesn't agree. "[65] The following events show this consistent behavior throughout time.

Jean Paul Sartre –accompanied by Simone de Beauvoir— [66] visited Cuba for a month during February and March 1960. The book he published later contains one of the earliest accounts of these traits of Castro's personality.[67] Sartre writes that Fidel became extremely upset when he received a warm soft drink in a rural tourist center where they had stopped. After "rummaging passionately around in a refrigerator that was out of order…" and being unable to fix it himself, he told the employees: "Tell your people in charge that if they don't take care of their problems, they will have problems with me." Sartre, like Dumont later, were appalled by Castro's wasting his time in this type of events.

Dumont[68] later recalled the first incident of this type Fidel had told him: "When I got the heads of the sixteenth zone together in Cienfuegos, I started by telling them: "Shut up, all of you, I came here to bawl you all out."" One of the leaders, who had spent the whole night there, had already told Dumont: "It was a real brawl".

In 1969, during the animal science event already discussed, Castro bluntly criticized the organizers because other state organizations were not present. He

---

64 Those not close to him –not accustomed to witness his outbursts– where able to watch it on live television in August 10, 1960. While delivering a speech at the CTC, a lady in the audience made an inaudible comment comparing the current with the former regime. Castro's swift reaction was reported in the newspapers. Castro attributed her action to either an intention to sabotage the meeting or because she has a mental problem. He ended the incident saying: "Rest assured that no one would dare to come here to provoke the people! No one in his senses would dare to do that!" (http://www.cuba.cu/gobierno/ discursos/1960/esp/f100860e.html).

65 Dumont (1970: 154, n 18).

66 Both were French writers and existentialist philosophers.

67 Sartre (1961: 122-123). See chapter "A day in the country with Fidel."

68 Dumont (1970: 54n30).

said: "Animal Science is not the only organism conducting research in agriculture. Other research is going on. No one has designated Animal Science as the Supreme Pontiff of agricultural research in Cuba."[69]

During the process of restructuring the sugar industry (see chapter 10), he confessed the circumstances when he had made that decision. He bluntly told a crowd of high-ranking administrators that his role was not to negotiate with ministers but to give orders to them.[70]

This behavior reveals Castro's reasons for the system of government he had chosen:[71] "We are not going to reproduce here the famous division of powers of the super-famous Montesquieu, now again in vogue... ¡there is one power, the people's power, and the revolution's power, that exercises the different functions!" Needless to say, that absolute power rested on his hands.

During the inaugural ceremony of a food cold-storage facility in 1991, Castro was discussing cost figures with the builders and managers. At some point, he told them in an authoritative manner: "... they are interesting figures that, for me to calculate, I demand the comrades to explain and explain clearly, and I don't like them to search for them in their little notebooks."[72]

In addition, there have been outbursts that show Castro's proprietary behavior in matters affecting Cuba's economy in general and its agricultural sector in particular.[73] Several events distant in time are very revealing.

In the early months of the revolution, he chided some guerrillas-turned-farmers over a tractor that was not operational: "Your apprenticeship is costing me very dearly."[74] A few years later, during the closing ceremony of the First National Sugar Forum, on September 19, 1964, he told the audience that, while

---

69 http://www.cuba.cu/gobierno/discursos/1969/esp/f130569e.html.

70 From his speech at the celebration of the 60th anniversary of Fidel Castro's admission to the University of Havana, November 17, 2005 (http://www.cuba.cu/gobierno/discursos/2005/ing/f171105i.html). His concern for conservation contrasts sharply with his launching of the Che Guevara Invading Brigade discussed below.

71 Castro (1991: 33).

72 http://www.cuba.cu/gobierno/discursos/1991/esp/f010491e.html.

73 See Hagelberg and Álvarez (2006: 134).

74 Otero (1960: 127).

conducting an experiment in a sugarcane field he had chosen, technicians from the electrical company arrived to erect a few towers for a high-voltage line. He complained and finally told the recent arrivals: "No, no, to destroy this field, you have to go over my dead body here!"[75] More than four decades later, the same attitude was present at Havana's annual trade fair: "Imagine how much we would have saved producing a smaller quantity of sugar. I'd prefer to cut a million and a half [tons] rather than 2 million, because with that million and a half we could have a reasonable profit".[76]

That many Cubans see Fidel as the country's owner was revealed in an encounter he had with a man in Manzanillo who had asked him for a house for him to live.[77] The man insisted ("But you can solve that for me") and Castro explained that there were others on the waiting list and he could not bypass them. If he asked the Commission in charge to do that, he would be acting as one of the Wise Men: "That would be the formula of the Wise Man and we can't behave as the wise men." In his refusal to behave as one, he is recognizing that he can do it, but will not. "It is not correct that you solve your problem because you had an encounter with me." Adding: "It is not with the Wise Man formula that the country's problems should be resolved, not solving the problem of one person, of anyone that we encounter on the road."

Dumont[78]refers to Castro finding a bridge in bad conditions and ordering that it be repaired immediately; his jeep getting stuck in the mud and telling his men to build a highway there; finding a dry area where crops were dying and ordering the building of a dam, etc.

His erratic behavior is another way of showing his sense of ownership. He may be a stubborn man. His opinion may be gospel, but he can change it as he pleases, as shown in the three issues discussed below (and expanded in the book's website): costs, windbreaks, and the sugar industry.

---

75 http://www.cuba.cu/gobierno/discursos/1964/esp/f190964e.html./
76 Dow Jones Newswires, 8 November 2003.
77 http://www.cuba.cu/gobierno/discursos/1966/esp/f260866e.html.
78 (1971: 167).

On July 7, 1963 he emphasized that, in agriculture, they had to think with an economic criterion, taking into account the problem of costs. By September 28, 1966, he had changed his position. He criticized those who had a dollar sign in the heart. But in July 16, 1976 he decided to implement a new economic model based on economic calculation.

Windbreaks was one of his favorite subjects, showing his complete support in speeches dated September 28, 1966, September 30, 1968 and January 5, 1969. Windbreak curtains were the solution to avoid or minimize damage from hurricanes. Until February 3, 1991 when he rejected the idea on the same basis he had supported it in the first place: windbreaks curtains had proven insect hosts and steal water and light from the crops.

The same process occurred with the sugar industry. On July 26, 1963, January 1, 1968, and December 20, 1969 he expressed his support for the main industry of the country. On a speech in November 17, 2005, he confessed to have called the sugar minister to order him to stop new plantings of sugarcane and start a process of restructuring. The alleged reason was high energy consumption but many believe it was the culmination of an anti-sugar feeling dating back to Colonial times.

Assuming the Leadership of his Own Opposition

Few observers of the Cuban reality have discovered this feature of Castro's leadership personality. It is not a common trait. Castro has shown the usefulness of becoming the leader of the opposition to his own regime on certain occasions.

Between 1976 and 1986 (as will be discussed later in chapter 3), the Cuban regime introduced a series of minor market reforms that were part of the System of Management and Planning of the Economy (SDPE). One of the policies concerning the agricultural sector was the opening of the Free Peasant Markets (*mercados libres campesinos*) in 1980.

Castro embraced the changes with enthusiasm. He delivered a speech at the graduating ceremony of economic technicians that would implement the new system. He referred constantly to the efficiency that the SDPE would promote and believed that his revolution had at last found the proper road. Criticisms

39

began to spread among some of the leaders.[79] They led to the removal in 1985 of Humberto Pérez, President of the Central Planning Board –the person in charge of implementing the SDPE. By that time, Castro's enthusiasm for the new system had turned sour. On December 2, 1986, during the Third Congress of the Cuban Communist Party, he criticized many of the changes that were occurring to institutionalize the Soviet functions along with the new economic model.[80] Castro condemned the free peasant markets. He said that it was painful to see garlic vendors selling garlic at very high price, only working a few hours a year.[81]

He played that role several times. Although brilliant in politics, one has to recognize that the most relevant characteristic of Castro's leadership has been his belief that Cuba is an expanded Birán. That feeling may explain part of his behavior concerning his decision-making in agriculture.

Birán: Fidel's Early Circumstance

Birán is a small hamlet located in the municipality of Mayarí, in the northern part of the former Oriente province. Birán is the rural community where the estate owned by the parents of Fidel and Raúl Castro was located. It is also the place of birth of the six children of Ángel Castro and Lina Ruz, including Fidel and Raúl.

---

79 Baloyra (1993: 52-53).
80 http://www.cuba.cu/gobierno/discursos/1986/esp/f021286e.html.
81 http://www.cuba.cu/gobierno/discursos/1986/esp/f021286e.html.

As the result of long conversations and subsequent research started during a trip to Birán in 1996, and right after his illness in 2006, Cuban journalist and writer Katiuska Blanco published three voluminous accounts of the Cuban leader's life and one about his father Ángel Castro. Although repetitive in many occasions, the exercise has expanded the one performed by Ignacio Ramonet in 2003-2005 and, in a more modest fashion, by Frei Betto in 1985. The subject matter of one of Blanco's early questions was Birán: "An ancient Indian proverb suggests, "Tell about your village and you'll tell about the world…" In your case, I have always thought, "Tell about Birán and you will unveil Fidel's soul and inspiration." "[82]

Blanco recalls what Castro had confessed to García Márquez with a whispering voice: "The school was my day care and Birán my Aracataca. "[83] Blanco's question allowed the Cuban leader to reveal the importance that his place of birth had in his life: "How do you remember the place, the friends, the forest, the trees, the workers of the *batey*,[84] the neighbors …? "[85]

The family house was like the hub of the village. One of Castro's friends[86] described it as a large country house, sordid, dirty, where he never saw a book, or a painting or a flower. For him, Birán was like a camp. In addition to the family house, there were warehouses, a general store, a small school, a post office with telegraph facilities, a liquor store and even a cockfighting ring that the Castro brothers would convert into a boxing ring during some weekends.[87] Castro's sister Juanita remembers Birán as a place where life was simple but had everything. There were the Castro warehouses –the store that was a supermarket--, the butcher shop across the store, and somewhat away and more secluded, although within the farm, the bakery that catered to the entire area.[88]

---

82 Blanco Castiñeira (2012: 18).

83 Aracataca is a municipality located in the Department of Magdalena, in Colombia's Caribbean, the place of birth of Gabriel García Márquez, 1982 Nobel Prize winner and Fidel Castro's close friend. He died in Mexico City on April 17, 2014.

84 Name given to the area around the sugar mills and large farms in the Antilles, where the houses, stores, warehouses, sugar production areas, and even the churches were located.

85 Blanco Castiñeira (2012: 19).

86 Pardo Llada (1988: 13, 14).

87 http://www.theguardian.com/travel/2010/jul/31/fidel-castro-family-home-cubalanco.

88 Juanita Castro (2009: 59).

The estate was a 23,000-acre plantation mainly devoted to sugarcane production, which yielded around 4 million arrobas (50,000 short tons) per season.[89] Castro states[90] that his father originally owned 2,000 acres and leased land from other owners until he controlled over 25,000 acres. His next-door neighbor, the United Fruit Co., by the 1950s possessed 330,000 acres—over 90 percent of the arable land in the Nipe Bay region.[91] Don Ángel kept excellent economic relations with his American neighbors, despite the commercial competition and the constant silent struggle about the boundaries of their respective farms.[92]

Those characteristics refer to the physical and geographical attributes of the place where they lived. However, there were other aspects of their daily lives more important than the surroundings. Some credible sources refer to rumors that Don Ángel advanced the fences of his farm at night to enlarge his holdings. Despite the outright denial of Juanita Castro,[93] several people (some close to the family) have testified to that fact. José Pardo Llada, once one of Fidel's best friends in the 1950s, who spent a six-day vacation with him in Birán, wrote that Don Ángel, after working for three years as a field foreman with the United Fruit Company, "became the owner of a 10,000-acre-farm, no one knows exactly how."[94] Carlos Franqui[95] questions Don Ángel's honesty, becoming so rich in such little time, based on what Fidel told him about the size of his father's *latifundia*. While researching and interviewing numerous people for her book, Geyer[96] came across testimonies confirming that Don Ángel "was far from meticulous about the manner in which he expanded his dominion. He would go out at night with his men on horseback, and in the dark they would "move the fences," thus always expanding his land into unclaimed areas."

---

89 Blanco (2003: 183).
90 Castro and Ramonet (2006: 28).
91 http://cabinetmagazine.org/issues/11/kushner.php.
92 Ibid., p. 154.
93 Juanita Castro (2009: 54).
94 Pardo Llada (1988: 11).
95 (1988: 17).
96 (1991: 22-23).

Observant as he has always been, Fidel Castro had to be aware of his father's practice. A famous historian goes to an extreme when stating that, besides his hard work, Ángel Castro "hacked his farm out of forest, perhaps sometimes on moonless nights, perhaps by stealing title deeds. "[97]

The general store has a story all by itself. Juanita Castro says that, under the shadow of a tree, his father "would write vouchers to all the residents of the area, authorizing them to buy what they needed in the store, for Christmas and New Year's dinners."[98] Blanco's book[99] shows a picture of the store with the legend: "Clothing and grocery store where Don Ángel issued vouchers to the peasants and workers of Birán." The description seems to indicate that Ángel Castro paid his employees with vouchers that had value only at his stores. No cash. No checks. No choice.

A photograph of a trolley line says it belonged to Don Ángel Castro, who used it to travel to Central Miranda and the city of Santiago de Cuba. Up front, it has a # 67 painted in white and the words "Angel Castro and Sons, Birán, Ote". [100] That, by itself, shows a degree of wealth and power very few people enjoyed in the rural Cuba of the 1920s and 1930s.

On that family farm, Fidel Castro spent his halcyon childhood. He returned happily to his enclave during school breaks and summer vacations. There exist numerous accounts of the importance that rural life may have had in the development of Castro's feelings and personality.[101]

Fidel Castro was always extremely happy in the rural environment of his parents' estate. Since early in his infancy, Castro became part of Birán. The sounds of roosters, pigs, cows, horses or dogs were familiar sounds for him.[102]

From his earliest years, Fidel Castro counted weapons as his most prized possessions —slingshots, bows and arrows, rifles, pistols, and shotguns. When

---

97　Thomas (1977: 18).
98　Juanita Castro (2009: 63).
99　Blanco (2003).
100　Blanco (2003).
101　See Blanco (2003).
102　Blanco, p. 85.

he was scarcely old enough to lift a shotgun, he took one into the backyard and blasted some chickens.[103] He fired his weapons at will with the silent consent of his father. No one told him what to do. He would come and go at any time. He was truly free in the familiar environment of his parents' estate and surrounding areas.

Fidel enjoyed wondering around the countryside. At the age of 12, Castro started going far away, to the forest or to the house of grandfather Don Pancho, about four kilometers from home. Everyone, from his father to every farm employee, respected his independence.[104] One of his favorite places was the Mayarí Pinewoods (*Pinares de Mayarí*). There were two paths to reach that location, one long, not too steep and meandering among hills; another short and dangerous, winding through high elevations. The young Fidel preferred the latter.[105]

Christmas breaks and Easter Week provided marvelous times to spend at home. Summer vacations were the best for he could swim in rivers, scamper through the woods, hunt with slingshots, ride horses. He felt free in contact with nature.[106]

A book published in Cuba,[107] after mentioning instances showing a godfather-like behavior, says: "Don Ángel kept his workers employed year-around, although this would entail carrying water from the river in the dry season. Don Ángel's men worked for twice the salary paid elsewhere, under the supervisor in charge. "[108] Fidel's close friend who spent a vacation in Birán, argued that the workers were paid starvation wages.[109] Fidel Castro himself, while speaking

---

103 Quirk (1993: 10).

104 Blanco, pp. 185-186.

105 Blanco, p. 173.

106 Betto (1985: 123).

107 In another book, the same author (Blanco Castiñeira 2008: 151) accuses the United Fruit Company of stealing land from its neighbors, ejecting farmers from their lots and exploiting its workers. The author asserts that Mr. Castro defended the workers from the Company's unfair practices.

108 Blanco (2003: 183).

109 Pardo Llada (1988: 13).

with an American photojournalist,[110] described his father in a curiously detached voice: "He had owned a large sugar plantation on the other side of the mountains. He had been a *latifundista*, a wealthy landowner who exploited the peasants. He had paid no taxes on his land or income. He had "played politics for money"."

However, during his interviews with Blanco,[111] Castro described a very generous father, one far from being a greedy person. Castro reiterated that don Ángel did not care much about money, savings or profits, because he was quite detached about money. His mother, on the contrary, criticized him because she was always very rigorous and defended with maternal instinct the management of money. The following event shows that side of Lina and an important one of Fidel.

Ramón, Angelita and Fidel became ill with a severe flu and someone recommended orange juice or decoction of the orange tree bark to relieve fever and breathlessness. But oranges were only available from a distant place. This created an unbearable delay for Don Ángel, who blamed himself for his lack of foresight.[112] When his children recovered, he decided to plant fifteen thousand orange trees –a gigantic project—for medicinal purposes. The back of the house soon showed an elegant and fragrant orchard, to which Ángel and Lina tended with special care.

Near the end of the guerrilla war, before marching into Santiago de Cuba, Fidel and his brother Raúl paid a visit to their mother in Birán on Christmas Eve 1958. Without regard for Lina's special care in harvesting the oranges with scissors, Fidel invited his troops and neighbors to the orchard (which did not belong to him, but perhaps beginning to feel a sense of ownership over the entire country), and a disorganized avalanche of people started pulling the fruit from the branches to Lina's dismay. Castro makes a startling confession: "Imagine, we had been nearly 25 months at war in the mountains, we had already exercised state functions, we had enacted an agrarian reform, laws of all kinds, had confiscated

---

110 Lockwood (1990: 16).
111 (2012: 36).
112 The story appears in Blanco (2003: 90, 399; 2012: 97-98).

herds of cattle and levied taxes on the country's sugar mills... I had almost lost the sense of formality."

His behavior and his words reveal that, without having achieved power yet, he was acting as Cuba's head of state on his parents' property. That very same night he told his brother Ramón: "This will be the first property to pass to state hands." Even before the triumph, Fidel Castro had developed that sense of ownership that would become more evident in the agricultural sector with the passing of time.

Searching for similar cases, one has to go back as far as the 1800s in Paraguay, where we find a dictator with deep interest in agriculture but with opposite results as Castro's. Dr. Gaspar Rodríguez de Francia ran the country between 1811 and 1840, with full dictatorial powers since 1814. "He imposed order, preached the gospel of hard work, and introduced improved methods in agriculture and stock rising. Under his rod, Paraguayans worked tirelessly, making the soil produce more than it ever had before. "[113] That has not been the case of Castro's Cuba.

Still another example involves Prime Minister Nikita Khrushchev. His behavior parallels Castro's for his insistence "upon telling the farms in one area to grow corn, and those in another area to grow peas, or to argue that science supported a particular type of cultivation."[114]

The final note is a weird parallel that came to mind while researching this topic. For Fidel Castro, and perhaps for the rest of the Castro siblings, Birán was a hidden paradise. His sister Juanita complains about its inaccessibility during the rainy season and the 700 kilometers they had to travel to get there from Havana during vacations. She recalls Fidel saying: "If Cuba is shaped like a crocodile, Birán for being so far, must be the butt." In a sense, Macondo –the village that García Márquez describes in *One hundred years of solitude*—is very similar to Birán. In addition to their isolation, both share the experience of the turmoil provoked by the arrival of the movies. In Macondo, it was the belief of the spectators that actors who had died in a previous film would not reappear in

---

113   http://www.latinamericanstudies.org/paraguay/paraguay-dictatorship.htm.
114   Laird and Laird (1970: 147).

future ones. Juanita Castro was the person who brought the fantasy of movies to Birán.[115] "Cine Juanita" opened with a Mexican film entitled *Juntos, pero no revueltos* [Together, but not mixed]. A small group of black neighbors complained. For them, the title implied that blacks and whites could not attend the functions together. The 15-year old owner Juanita came out to talk to the protesting blacks and the problem was solved.

The dialogue approach of his sister Juanita was not one of Castro's problem-solving methods when dealing with Cuba's agricultural issues. His personality traits, shaped partially by his life in Birán, along with the enormous power he wielded, help one understand his subsequent role as czar of the agricultural sector. Max Weber[116] stated that charismatic leadership can be established and maintained only through success. In Fidel Castro's case, his successful political adroitness (a result of his charisma, narcissism and *caudillismo*) tend to support Weber's thesis, while the opposite is true in the case of his agricultural follies.

---

115 Juanita Castro (2009: 64-67).
116 See Suárez (1971: 4).

Chapter 3

THE SEARCH FOR AN ECONOMIC MODEL

Marxism is many things. It is a way to know the world,
a critique of the world, and a means to change the world.[1]

efore exploring the nature and outcomes of Fidel Castro's agricultural experiments, the reader must be aware of the evolution of Cuba's search for an economic model, including agriculture.

1959-1960:
The Short-Lived Humanistic Revolution

Repeatedly in the early months of the revolution, Fidel Castro declared that it was of a humanistic nature, vaguely defined as "freedom with bread; bread without terror. "[2] On April 15, 1961, on the eve of the Bay of Pigs invasion he declared the socialist nature of the revolution and, on December 2 of that year, specified its Marxist-Leninist ideology. In less than three years, Castro had defined and redefined his revolution from humanism to a generic form of socialism to the ideology known as scientific socialism. The fact that Marx did not leave an implementation handbook offered an excellent opportunity for the innovative and daring mind of the young revolutionary. During 1959-1961, he was building the foundations of a regime he would manage caudillo style for the next several decades.[3]

---

1 McGuire (2008: 73).

2 http://www.cuba.cu/gobierno/discursos/1959/esp/f240459e.html.

3 Most of what follows was summarized from Álvarez (1990).

1961-1966:
Two Very Distinct Systems

During the 1961-1966 period, two systems of economic organization, management and finance coexisted as two different approaches of first building socialism and later communism. The Centralized Budgetary System of Finance, or *Sistema Presupuestario de Financiamiento* (SPF), whose main ideologue was Ernesto Guevara, operated mainly in the state industrial sector. The Self-Finance System (SFS) prevailed in the agricultural and foreign trade sectors, and in some parts of the industrial sector.

The SPF was highly centralized. It did not make use of commercial relations or material incentives. Enterprises and production units were financed by the state budget. The main feature of the SFS was the relative degree of autonomy enjoyed by the enterprises and production units. The central authority developed a national economic plan and the units were responsible for their own financing. To some extent, the SFS made use of market mechanisms and, in contrast with the SPF, it advocated the use of material incentives to foster labor productivity. The debate between the proponents of the two models included topics such as the relationship with the Soviet Union, the role of labor unions and the Party, and the need for institutionalization, among others. It was obvious that Castro –who remained conspicuously silent during the debate—was not going to tolerate such a debate for long as he believed in the need of a unique system for all sectors of the economy.

In a speech on September 28, 1966, Fidel Castro directly denounced economic and financial scrutiny of the government's policies:[4] "A financier, a pure economist, a metaphysician of the Revolution, would have said, "Careful! Do not lower those rents by one cent, because financially, because economically, because more pesos, fewer pesos." Those persons have a peso sign in their heads and want the people also to have a peso sign in their heads and in their hearts. In addition, if we want that the people get rid of the peso sign in the mind and the heart, then we must have men who free their thought of the peso sign."

---

4 In the 6th anniversary of the CDR, Revolution Square, 28 September 1966. http://www. cuba.cu/gobierno/discursos/1966/esp/f280966e.html. Also published in *Cuba Socialista*, No. 62, October 1966.

Those words heralded the implementation of a new system of managing the economy that departed from the traditional approach of the Soviet bloc concerning the building of socialism first and communism later.

1966-1970:
Decentralized Budgetary System

In 1966, Castro defined the new goal of building socialism and communism simultaneously by means of a new approach: the Decentralized Budgetary System or, in Cuban terms, *Sistema de Registro*.

Fidel Castro disclosed the new idea during a speech to the central workers' union, claiming the right to develop his own methods.[5] He argued that new situations were present and the Cubans had the right to think with their own heads in the task of building socialism and communism. Since that is an entirely new approach and there is no handbook on how to do so, they had the right to do it with their own means, procedures and methods. Then, he spelled out the revisionist road: "We will build socialism and communism and we shall overcome."

To prove his commitment, he announced a series of new measures: commodity prices would reflect social function rather than costs of production; therefore, the prices of many goods and services were lowered and many were offered free. The Ministry of Finance disappeared and the National Bank had its power reduced. The allocation of resources without utilizing market mechanism was another important measure. Further policies took effect in the following months: economic records replaced the accounting system kept by banks and enterprises and all written monetary transactions among state enterprises ceased; taxes and interest on banks credit disappeared along with the national budget. In a mind-boggling decision, production was to take place without regard for costs. In the ideological arena, all universities and Communist Party schools stopped teaching courses dealing with the political economy of socialism and all major theoretical journals ceased publication. The discipline of public accounting disappeared from universities' curriculum.

---

5 On August 29, 1966. http://www.cuba.cu/gobierno/discursos/1966/esp/f290866e.html.

Other measures included lowering the price of many goods and services and offering many for free; sports events, new housing, public telephones, childcare centers, and even birthday cakes and funerals were provided free of charge. In the countryside, members of experimental communities received free housing and electricity and their children's clothing, shoes and food in neighborhood schools was also offered at no cost.

While addressing a group of youth during the inauguration of a dam in the Isle of Pines, on August 12, 1967, Castro told them:[6] "The youth here must have the task of revolutionizing nature. Also in the social order, what is the goal, what is the ideal of those contingents of young people who move here? What kind of life do you think should be the life of men and women who live in this region? Why not convert also the area in the first communist region of Cuba?"

He became a preacher of the new approach. During a graduation ceremony held on December 9, 1967, he touched on the subject in the following manner:[7] "That is what is called communism and it is something that is beyond socialism. In addition, it is not just a problem of development of material wealth, but and most essentially, a problem of development of human consciousness." On January 6, 1968, during the inauguration of a new town in Havana's Green Belt he stated:[8] "That is, our society is serious about moving towards communist distribution."

Along the same line was his speech at the anniversary of the March 13, 1957 events, held at the University of Havana on the same day in 1968.[9] He announced a "revolutionary offensive" intended to do away with the remaining vestiges of private property on the island, especially the so-called "timbiriches" or small street kiosks that sold all sorts of things, especially food products. After his announcement, he touched on the controversial subject of stimuli. For a long time, according to him, stimuli were a theoretical subject matter and thought to be a matter of methodology but, in his opinion, it was a much deeper issue. To

6 http://www.cuba.cu/gobierno/discursos/1967/esp/f120867e.html.
7 http://www.cuba.cu/gobierno/discursos/1967/esp/f091267e.html.
8 http://www.cuba.cu/gobierno/discursos/1968/esp/f060168e.html.
9 http://www.cuba.cu/gobierno/discursos/1968/esp/f130368e.html.

him, material incentives were in contradiction with the building of a communist society.

The new approach was in full operation by the end of 1968. The political battle had been won, but economic performance had failed. Castro then played the role of leader of the opposition within his own government –a common practice during his tenure. Before returning to the drawing board, it was necessary to correct the costly mistakes of this period. That was the objective of 1970-1976, known as the process of institutionalization of the revolution.

1970-1976:
The Institutionalization of the Revolution

The end of the Decentralized Budgetary System coincided with the failure to reach the goal of 10 million metric tons of sugar. The country was in need of social and institutional reforms, that required a new economic model.

Among the changes implemented were a new constitution; a new family code; the creation of local and national assemblies of popular power; a new judicial system; and a redefinition of political-administrative boundaries within the country.

The realization that socialism and communism could not be built simultaneously meant ending some previous policies, especially those granting free goods and services to the population. The new approach returned economic policies closer to the experiences of the Soviet Union and Eastern Europe. Fidel Castro approved the new model and his role as head of the state and the Party was unchallenged.

1976-1985:
Economic Management and Planning System

The new economic model was the Economic Management and Planning System or *Sistema de Dirección y Planificación de la Economía* (SDPE). The official announcement was made at the first congress of the Cuban Communist Party (PCC) in December 1975. A few months later, Castro spoke to graduates of courses on implementation of the SDPE:[10] "Implementing the Economic Management and Planning System will take a number of years, and its essential objective is the efficiency of economic activity: learning to get the most from every penny and every ounce of raw material... That is what we want: efficiency!"

This time the change represented a gigantic leap, from zero consideration of costs to the application of the "law of value." Castro declared that, among the important tasks to perform were "the partial recovering of economic controls and the emphasis on cost accounting and cost reduction." The SDPE, he said, recognized the existence of "the law of value," and the need "to determine, to the last detail, how much we spend in everything we produce..."[11]

As customary, gigantism took over in preparing the technicians who would train others in the application of the new system.[12] Fidel Castro mentioned that his goal was that the school founded by the recent graduates would become an important and decisive institution of the country: The number of students was high: 358 enrolled in the course of economic technicians, 239 in courses to form the leaders of the economy, 169 registered in the course for professors and 135 in the one for administrators. The total is more than 800 students. He said that, except for two provinces, similar schools would be established in all Cuban provinces because they needed to prepare one technician for each of the country's 4,000 enterprises.

The SDPE rested on four operational principles: 1) Self-financing by each enterprise with a profit objective: each enterprise, after covering costs, must show a positive difference. 2) Operational economic independence by the enterprise. 3) Each individual worker should be concerned with the enterprise's economic activity. The system allowed for both material and moral incentives. 4) Monetary control of the enterprise by the financial and banking institutions (control through the peso).

---

10   In the closing ceremony of two courses of the National School for management of the economy, Havana, July 16, 1976: http://www.cuba.cu/gobierno/discursos/1976/esp/f160776e.html.

11   http://www.cuba.cu/gobierno/discursos/1977/esp/f170577e.html.

12   The figures appear in Castro's speech at http://www.cuba.cu/gobierno/discursos/1976/esp/f160776e.html.

José Álvarez, Ph.D.

1986-1991:
Process of Rectification of Errors and Negative Tendencies

While the SDPE was in operation, some of the leaders expressed criticisms. The failure to recognize that the source of problems was the planning process itself, and not the person in charge of implementing it, led to the removal in 1985 of Humberto Pérez, President of the Central Planning Board.

By that time, Castro's enthusiasm for the new system had turned into opposition. On December 2, 1986, during the Third Congress of the Cuban Communist Party, he criticized the institutionalization process along with the new economic model.[13] He referred to two types of illusions that had been created: The first was the belief that the state would function smoothly after the enactment of the Constitution, and the establishment of the political and administrative division of the country and the organs of Popular Power. The other illusion was the belief that everything would go perfectly under the SDPE, "with the linking of pay and work, the panacea that would solve everything and very nearly going to build socialism."

Castro listed a multitude of "errors and negative tendencies" (the name of his new campaign against his own government) as the result of the SDPE application. They included: the organization of work and salaries; labor discipline; resource allocation and utilization; work style; the demands and control by the Party in the different organizations; problems with the cadres; ideological, social and youth problems; problems with the peasantry; the depletion of resources; the use of money to solve all problems, and several others. He turned again against the practice of economic calculation and argued about the impossibility of applying the system in the area of public health services. His example was the challenge posed by calculating the profitability of a hospital and the return on the investment.

---

13 http://www.cuba.cu/gobierno/discursos/1986/esp/f021286e.html.

The economic model dismissed had yet to have a substitute. Many years later, an evaluation of what followed had been set out:[14] "From one day to the next, the country was without a model, without a governing principle for its economic activity, but the worst was that an alternative system was not proposed. Then someone took out of the trunk of memories Ernesto Guevara's budgetary system... while the country's economy was inexorably going into the abyss... At the end, all came to nothing and the country continued under the baton of the "Alchemist"."

What followed was the opposite of what would happen in most political regimes. Castro's leadership and ideas continued to be undisputable. Subsequently, Fidel Castro showed one of his personality traits. After trying several approaches, and failing in all, including the economic calculation methodology of the Soviet bloc since the early phases of socialism, Fidel Castro considered his moral duty to inform the other socialist countries that they had been wrong all along because the implementation of that model failed in Cuba. He explained how he had done it at the 70th anniversary of the October Revolution when he headed the Cuban delegation to the celebrations. He explained that event at the inaugural session of the IV Congress of the Cuban Communist Party, held in Heredia Theater in Santiago de Cuba on October 10, 1991:[15] Castro criticized the implementation of the SDPE and alerted his colleagues about not joining the new currents of glasnost and perestroika. With a complete lack of humility, he informed: "They listened to me with great interest and, indeed, many of them told me later: "Hey, the same has happened to us. "... I fulfilled my historical duty to warn them at least not to follow those tendencies; not to fall into the temptation of copying capitalism, and on that occasion, my words were heard very well."

Castro's speech was sandwiched between two crucial events. On November 9, 1989, the world had witnessed the fall of the Berlin Wall. A few weeks after his speech –and everyone saw it coming—the Soviet Union formally dissolved by Decree of December 26, 1991. He was already preparing measures to attempt

---

14 "El modelo cubano está agotado" [The Cuban model is exhausted], posted by Frank Álvarez at http://www.conexioncubana.net/somoscuba/el-modelo-cubano-esta-agotado/

15 http://www.cuba.cu/gobierno/discursos/1991/esp/f101091e.html.

to survive in a world with no support from the Soviet Union and the rest of the socialist bloc.

1991 - ?:
Inventing in the Post-Soviet Era

The Cuban regime announced the establishment of a "Special Period in Times of Peace" to deal with the absence of subsidies from the former socialist countries. Many measures to save resources were implemented and the country lived its worst period of scarcity since 1959.

The new economic situation would not stop Castro's leadership in Cuba's agricultural sector. His main efforts were devoted to a gigantic Food Plan that also resulted in a dramatic failure. Fidel Castro fell ill and, on 31 July 2006, his brother assumed the duties of President of Cuba's Council of State in a temporary transfer of power. On February 24, 2008, the National Assembly of People's Power unanimously chose General Raúl Castro as Fidel's permanent successor.

Since this book deals with Fidel Castro's leadership in the agricultural sector, the process of reforms and counter-reforms initiated by Raúl Castro after replacing his brother is not included.[16]

---

16 Mesa-Lago (2012) and Mesa-Lago and Pérez-López (2013) are excellent sources.

Chapter 4

THE LOUSY RESULTS AND THE SCAPEGOATS

Can one play like so with the destiny of a nation?
Did anyone authorize him to undertake these insane... ventures?
Did he consult the people in any way?
26 of July's No. 1 Manifesto to the people of Cuba, Mexico, 8 August 1955.

A Few Words on Performance

Since the first of his *"Reflexiones del Comandante en Jefe"* appeared on March 28, 2007, I have been tempted to suggest him to write one about his performance as caudillo of Cuba's agricultural sector. (An honest one, *Comandante*. You must write a Reflection that does not blame your failures on the usual culprits.)

The following chapters describe some of his follies. The problem is that very few of them are quantifiable. Since numbers are so important to judge the success or failure of a project, I tried to find as many statistics as I could. They have the limitation of being in different currencies for different years, but at least they provide an overall picture of the costs of some of these plans. They can be studied in the website of this book (www.cubanquixote.com).

Other methods are appropriate to evaluate Castro's performance as an agricultural manager. Table 4.1 illustrates one of those methods. Because the population has almost doubled since Castro took power in 1959, the statistics appear in kilograms per capita. Two economists living on the island developed the Table. The comparison between 1958 and the averages of 1975-79 and 1986-89 avoid including in the averages the negative impact of the Special Period on the Cuban economy. The numbers speak for themselves.

Table 4.1 Agricultural and livestock production in Cuba, 1958, average 1975-79, and average 1986-89.

Commodity	1958	Average (1975-79)	Average (1986-89)
		(kg/capita)	
Corn	31.50	1.75	3.50
Beans	5.68	0.38	1.31
Tubers & roots	114.4	45.93	63.45
Tobacco	7.41	4.39	3.97
Coffee	6.43	2.12	2.60
Plantains	37.09	22.81	29.89
Other fruits	59.9	39.4	30.90
Livestock	0.83	0.52	0.40
Pork	0.26	0.08	0.12

Notes: For 1958 agricultural production: (CEE) Cuba, Desarrollo Económico y Social durante el período 1958-80, December 1981, p. 194. FAO data for beans and plantains. The figure for livestock in 1958 was estimated by Raúl Cepero Bonilla: Los problemas de la agricultura de América Latina y la reforma agraria cubana. Cuba Socialista, 3 1993, p. 91. The averages for 1975-79 and 1986-89 were computed from Anuario Estadístico de Cuba, 1981, 1988 and 1989.

Source: Manuel Sánchez Herrero and Arnaldo Ramos Lauzurique. *Los llamados "logros"*. La Habana, 1998 (See complete article at http://www.futurodecuba.org/los_llamados.htm).

Besides the figures in Table 4.1, it is necessary to investigate the performance of the "import dependency ratio", which measures the percentage of food imports needed to satisfy the consumption of the population. Official Cuban sources reported figures of 31% in 1954, 23.3% in 1955 and 20.7% in 1956.[1] The current estimate by the World Food Program of the United Nations

---

1   As reported by Nova González (1993: 76).

puts the figure at 80%.[2] Other sources confirm it.[3] One of them dates back to 2008.[4]

In an article about food imports as economic indicators, the author states: "The pulse of Cuba's agricultural success cannot be taken by considering food import figures alone. Those numbers are often misleading, and one must maintain a broad understanding of Cuba and what the farming community is capable of producing given its political, social and geographic restrictions. "[5] The numbers below should answer that author's concern. They are the response to Castro's constant reference to Cuba becoming the top producer in an infinite list of agricultural commodities. The degree to which those predictions failed is shown by the following figures (commodity followed by rank) released in 2008, at the time of the transfer of power from Fidel to his brother Raúl Castro. Their source is FAOSTAT, Food and Agricultural Organization of the United Nations, Country rank in the world, by commodity:[6]

Yautía (cocoyam): 6; Agave fiber nes: 14; mango pulp: 18; Juice, mango: 18; Bastfibres: 21; Yams: 27; Grapefruit (including pomelos): 29; Milk, whole condensed: 32; Pumpkins, squash and gourds: 32; Plantains: 32; Sisal: 35; Papayas: 35; Coconuts, desiccated: 37; Sugar cane, raw Centrifugal: 38; Bagasse: 39; Feed, pulp of fruit: 39; Raw sugar, centrifugal: 52; Cocoa, beans: 52; Garlic: 53; Beverages, distilled alcohol: 54; Cucumbers and gherkins: 54; Milk, whole evaporated: 54; Tobacco, unmanufactured: 56; Pinapples: 57; Dregs from brewing, distillation: 57; Beans, dry: 58; Cassava: 58; Bananas: 59; Chillies and peppers, green: 59; Tomatoes: 60; Oranges: 61; Cabbage and other brassicas: 63. Not one single first place!

The top 50 Cuban agricultural export products and commodities show a dismal performance at the time Castro ceded power to his brother.

Let us explore an additional reason —not mentioned frequently—for the failure. For years, Fidel Castro claimed that Cuba's large state farms were the

---

2   http://www.wfp.org/countries/cuba.

3   http://en.wikipedia.org/wiki/Agriculture_in_Cuba.

4   "Cuban leader looks to boost food production". CNN. April 17, 2008.

5   Gifford (2010: 49).

6   http://faostat.fao.org/site/339/default.aspx.

"superior form of agricultural organization." Even foreign sympathizers have cast doubts about the veracity of that statement.[7]

How wide is the gap between the state and non-state sectors? There are different estimates from authors inside and outside Cuba about the failure of this type of organization. In Cuba, Nova González[8] has shown that, since 1979 or 1980, but especially since 1986, Cuba's agricultural and livestock activities in general experienced production declines, loss of efficiency, and/or stagnation in key production areas. That happened despite the strong capital investment that took place during the 1980s, the decade of the extensive growth model.

Outside of Cuba, a larger study revealed startling results.[9] The authors tested the hypothesis that non-state farms performed better than state farms during the decades of the 1970s and 1980s in volume and quality of output despite an unequal access to factors of production and other resources. Briefly, these are some of the results of the study:

- Non-state farms' production surpassed state units during each of the 21 sugar campaigns between 1969 through 1989. Private farmers accounted for 17.9% of harvested areas but produced 19.3% of total output, resulting from higher yields. That productivity advantage would have resulted in an average extra *zafra* every 10 years. Furthermore, and *ceteris paribus,* if the non-state sector had operated all state sugarcane lands during the period under study,[10] the advantage in productivity would have translated in an average "extra" *zafra* every four years.

- Beans, and tubers and roots, appear to show opposite results. Since the statistics include only those commodities moving through *Acopio* (the state collection agency), and they are not perishable, farmers keep them for consumption or sales in the black market.

- Tomatoes are perishable commodities that have to move fast. The non-state sector produced more than its share of area planted.

---

7   Benjamin et al. (1986: 180).
8   1994.
9   Álvarez and Puerta (1994).
10   Calculated from 1989 Anuario Estadístico de Cuba, p. 188.

- Tobacco presents similar shares in both planted area and average yields. The crop receives special attention and processing facilities are necessary before consumption.

Despite the facts demonstrating that Fidel Castro is the main responsible for the decrease in food consumption of his people, he was recognized by UN-FAO for reducing hunger in Cuba.

Rome, April 29, 2013

Dear Commander:

I have the honor to address you in my capacity as Director-General of the United Nations Organization for Food and Agriculture (FAO), to sincerely congratulate you and all the Cuban people for having fulfilled the goal set in advance by the World Food Summit, held in Rome in November 1996, and that proposed to halve the number of undernourished people in each country by the year 2015.

As you may recall, you honored us with his presence in that Summit and delivered a brief but powerful speech, which still lingers in the collective memory of our Organization. You concluded by saying: "the bells that toll today for those who die of hunger every day, will toll tomorrow for humanity if it refused, failed or could not be wise enough to save them." And they say that you said in the press conference that followed the Summit that even if the target were achieved we would not know what to say to the other half of humanity if it would not be freed from the scourge of hunger. They are concepts that until today still retain its meaning and value.

It's been 17 years since then and now I have the great pleasure to inform you that the decision of its members and for the first time in its history, the FAO Conference, to be held next June in Rome, take the total eradication hunger as the number one goal of our Organization.

At that time, we will pay a tribute to Cuba and 15 other countries that have been most successful in reducing hunger. To all of them we will give a certificate of recognition for having met the target of the Summit in advance. [Countries are mentioned]

Besides reiterating my congratulations on the significant success achieved by your country, I wish you well-being and success for you and all the Cuban people.

Yours with great esteem and appreciation,

José Graziano da Silva

The Incalculable Costs

Lack of data hinders the calculation of a benefit-cost ratio. Cost-benefit analysis is a formal discipline intended to evaluate the economic feasibility of projects. A benefit-cost ratio is an indicator that attempts to summarize the overall value of a project or proposal relative to its costs. Both costs and benefits should appear in discounted present values. Ratios over one generally represent a good investment.[11]

Besides the lack of cost data, when available, they are in Cuban pesos (of different dates), US dollars, rubles or CUCs. A Consumer Price Index that could be used to convert local currencies at current prices to a constant price is not available in Cuba. And so on. However, some cost information, as indicated above, is available in the book's website (www.cubanquixote.com), which shows a very small part of the huge expenses that these projects conveyed.

His brother Raúl, however, perhaps with no intention on passing judgment on Fidel's agricultural performance, did so soon after inheriting temporarily his functions and power. While addressing the crowd gathered in Camagüey on July 26, 2007 to commemorate another anniversary of the Moncada assault, he referred to one of his brother's agricultural priorities with total sarcasm: "I came by land to see that everything is green and beautiful, but the most beautiful thing, that which most caught my eye, was how pretty the *marabú* is all along the highway."[12]

Fidel had promised to get rid of that weed on multiple occasions. On August 30, 1966 he affirmed: "Next year our agriculture will make a tremendous effort toward eradicating … *marabú* from pastures."[13] Two years later, while visiting

---

11 http://en.wikipedia.org/wiki/Benefit%E2%80%93cost_ratio.

12 http://www.granma.cu/granmad/secciones/raul26/).

13 http://www.cch.kcl.ac.uk/legacy/teaching/av1000/textanalysis/castro/castro3.txt.

Havana's green belt on January 6, 1968 he said: "I understand that we have here the brigade that was going to work on the elimination of *marabú* on the outskirts of Havana. Last September 28 it was said that no *marabú* would be left in a year… but it looks that by the month of March there won't be any left in the outskirts of Havana."[14] Furthermore, the gigantic effort and huge expenses of the Che Guevara Invading Brigade (see chapter 7) were considered a failure by Cuba's current President.

The Alleged Culprits

How we love to blame others for our misfortunes!
Hardly one loser has the manliness to say frankly, I was wrong.[15]
B.C. Forbes.

The quote by the founder of *Forbes Magazine*, a leading source for reliable business news and financial information, is an excellent opener for this chapter. It is impossible to expect a *Mea culpa* from Fidel Castro for the destruction of Cuba's economy. His personal traits hinder the process of repentance. The way out is to look for other culprits. He has found three: the United States' policy against Cuba, Mother Nature and the crumbling of the Berlin Wall.

---

14 http://www.cuba.cu/gobierno/discursos/1968/esp/f060168e.html.
15 http://thoughts.forbes.com/thoughts/quotes/blame.

The United States' Policy against Cuba

It may have been true in some or many occasions, but the fact remains that the Cuban regime has blamed almost <u>all</u> of its failures on the United States of America. It does not matter if it is the economic embargo (that they call "block-ade") or real or alleged actions by the Central Intelligence Agency (CIA). Cuban officials have constantly reiterated that the agricultural sector has been a priority target of U.S. aggressions against their regime.

It is true that, in the early years of the revolution, when Cuba confiscated US properties and the latter responded with the suspension of the Cuban sugar quota and later by enforcing an economic embargo on the island, the Cuban economy –especially its agricultural sector—suffered from the lack of spare parts and other supplies that used to come from the North. However, little by little, Cuba started commercial relations with more countries than ever before. Above all, Cuba became a member of the socialist bloc and received huge subsidies that more than compensated for the loss of the benefits derived from trading with the United States. More than fifty years after arriving in power, the Cuban regime continues to blame "Yankee imperialism" for most of its malaises in the countryside. The government of the United States (there have been 11 Presidents and 19 Administrations from 1959 to 2014) has been the favorite scapegoat for the failures of an inefficient system of production and distribution.

It would not be honest to compare Cuba's embargo with two of the hardest true blockades in modern history, those against Spain's Francisco Franco (1944-1955) and South Africa (1985-1988). Spain was subject to a total blockade for its alliance with Fascism and Nazism. South Africa 's justification was its system of apartheid. These two countries not only resisted, but also were able to experience economic development and growth.

At present, the U.S. embargo on Cuba, which limits American businesses from dealing with Cuban interests, is still in effect and is the most enduring trade embargo in modern history. That said, the data show a very revealing opposite side.

Those who visit the United Census' website,[16] find that the United States is one of Cuba's top ten trading partners. The dollar value of direct sales from the U.S. to Cuba during the period 2004 to 2013 exceeded US$4.35 billion. Due to Cuba's reputation and low credit rating, all transactions have to be paid in cash before the purchases are shipped to the island. Furthermore, the United States has been Cuba's biggest donor of humanitarian aid, including medicines and medical supplies for decades.[17]

A stiff blockade would not allow sending family remittances to Cuba. The figure reported is close to US$2 billion annually. Most of that money is sent from the United States.[18]

A total blockade would tend to prohibit tourism to the punished country. However, there was a record number of people visiting Cuba from the United States in 2013: 200,000 legal visitors, although Global Travel Industry reports that another 300,000 Americans visited the island illegally. Those 500,000 visitors can be compared with the 180,000 tourists from the United States and the 20 to 30 thousand from Canada and Europe during the 1950s. Payments for the legal documents that Cubans living abroad need to travel to the island represent another source of income that ranges between 125 and 200 millions of CUC annually.[19]

Another fact that proves the absence of an embargo is the permission to pay in the United States for the use of cellular phones in Cuba. In 2010, 730,000 Cubans were using this technology paid for by their family members and relatives living in the United States. The income from this source in 2009 was of about US$216 million.[20]

One still needs to add the gift parcels that Cubans living abroad send their family members with unbelievable frequency. When added to the baggage

---

16 http://www.census.gov/foreign-trade/balance/c2390.html.

17 http://pjmedia.com/blog/the-cuban-embargo-myth/.

18 http://globedia.com/cuba-economia-hunde-remesas-crecen.

19 http://globedia.com/cuba-economia-hunde-remesas-crecen.

20 http://globedia.com/cuba-economia-hunde-remesas-crecen.

carried by travelers, whose 44-pound limit has been eliminated,[21] the amount of these transfers runs in the millions of dollars per month.

Despite the former facts, the accusations against US aggressions against Cuba have reached ridiculous tones in some occasions. In 1990, Castro accused the United States of trying to deflect hurricanes, and he suspected that was accomplished a few times. He also added that the Pentagon was conducting experiments to see if they could make the clouds discharge their water on the sea without reaching Cuba.[22]

Back in 1980 and 1981, Castro had accused the United States of not only considering the use of biological weapons against Cuba, but also of sending several plagues to the island. These were his words during his speech at the inauguration of the health complex "Ernesto Che Guevara":[23] "We have been successful in the struggle against the swine fever, successes in controlling the foci, our country is the only one achieving that... and this is the second time that we face that disease." Later, he states: "We have studied the chemicals to face the tobacco plague and it is very suspicious, so many plagues at the same time, when we know that the imperialists were planning many times and testing to utilize the means of bacteriological warfare against our country."

He returned to the topic months later during his speech commemorative of the Moncada assault in Las Tunas province, on July 26, 1981, stating that the conspiracy had started back in 1969 with hearing in the U.S. Congress. He referred to four harmful plagues that Cuba had suffered in the previous two years (the African swine fever, sugarcane rust, tobacco blue mold, and the dengue virus), which he believed were introduced by the Central Intelligence Agency of the United States.[24] In the last case, however, he recognized that "the high level of infestation of *Aedes Aegypti* due to the neglect of our sanitary authorities, were offering the incentive for such criminal sabotage against the health of our people.[25]

---

21 http://cubantriangle.blogspot.com/2009/09/obamas-new-rules-on-gift-parcels-to.html.
22 Castro (1990: 441).
23 http://www.cuba.cu/gobierno/discursos/1980/esp/f140680e.html.
24 http://www.cuba.cu/gobierno/discursos/1981/esp/f260781e.html.
25 Castro (1990: 440-441).

Mother Nature: Droughts and Hurricanes

There is a long list of statements by Castro and other public officials blaming the weather (mainly droughts and hurricanes) for failures of the agricultural sector. A sample follows:[26]

> … what was that forced us to pay attention to the water works problem? It was the drought phenomenon, the tremendous drought that took place in the years 1961 and 1962. (Fidel Castro).[27]

> Our farmers cannot continue at the mercy of hurricanes, of floods, of droughts. Our work cannot depend on whether or not it rains. (Fidel Castro).[28]

> Unless we conquer nature, nature will conquer us (Fidel Castro).[29]

> We have heavy damage to our sugarcane from the drought… We have pushed back the start of the [2000-2001] harvest a bit to allow the cane to benefit a little more from the rain. (Minister of Sugar Ulises Rosales del Toro).[30]

> Given the reduction in cane yield caused by the drought, the [2000-2001] harvest, which is about to begin, will result in lower production than the last [harvest] (Vice-President Carlos Lage).[31]

---

26 Part of the material in this segment comes from Álvarez (2003): http://www.ascecuba.org/publications/proceedings/volume13/pdfs/alvarez.pdf
27 (1990, p. 282).
28 (1990, p. 284).
29 (1992, p. 71).
30 "Current Developments" (2000: 18).
31 "Current Developments" (2000: 18).

Due to the embargo, and to adverse climatic conditions, production of vegetables and of meat from cattle, pigs and fowl decreased [in 1999-2000]. (Minister of Agriculture Alfredo Jordán).[32]

These foreign specialists used both excuses –droughts and hurricanes— simultaneously:

First all of, Cuban agriculture performed more poorly during 1985 and 1986. This was principally attributable to two factors: (1) there was an intensifying *drought* from 1983 through 1986; by 1986, rainfall was 35 percent below the historical average, and (2) in November 1985, Cuba experienced its most devastating hurricane since the revolution.[33]

In an attempt at elucidating a potential disparity between natural disasters before and after the revolution, I conducted a study comparing two sets of 43 years each: 1915-1958 and 1959-2002.[34] Data on cold fronts, floods and droughts were examined. The statistical analysis reached the following results: 1) There is no definitive proof that nature has been more damaging in either period. 2) In terms of the number of hurricanes, the 1915-1958 period experienced more brushes or passing of hurricanes than the following period. Hurricanr frequency, however, was higher in the second period. Both results convey statistical significance. 3) During the socialist period, it is easier to prepare for, and recover from, those disasters. The current civil defense system may be the reason. However, I did not even explore the recovery from the loss of financial resources.

The Crumbling of the Berlin Wall

The process of *glasnost* and *perestroika* produced an unprecedented unrest in the Socialist bloc that led to the falling of the Berlin Wall in the weeks following November 9, 1989. Allied governments began to fall one after the other. In

---

32 Zúñiga (2000: 1).
33 Zimbalist and Brundenius (1991: 250, 258).
34 Álvarez (2003).

Cuba, Fidel Castro saw the thunderstorm coming. During his speech commemorating the Moncada assault, held in the city of Camagüey on July 26, 1989, he stated the need to be realistic and, in the event that the USSR would disintegrate, Cuba could continue fighting and resisting.[35]

The impact on the Cuban economy could not have been more brutal and comprehensive, precisely because of the degree of dependence that had developed through the years. Fidel Castro had just found a third culprit: "It will be better understood if you take into account the terrible blow that our country has suffered with the socialist disaster, disaster over which we have no responsibility whatsoever."[36]

In summary, as was the case with Spain and South Africa, it is not only possible to resist economic sanctions but it may be even an incentive to bring about economic growth. Castro's regime has not generate growth. Every year, Mother Nature hits many countries of the world by means of not only freezes and hurricanes, but also earthquakes, tsunamis, volcano eruptions and other events worse than those experienced by Cuba. Eventually, those countries recover while Cuba continues to fall behind the rest of the world. Finally, it has been a quarter of a century since the dissolution of the Council for Mutual Economic Assistance and many of the former members are today well ahead of Cuba in terms of per capita income and other variables that measure growth and human satisfaction. For example, Slovakia is a high-income economy with the highest sustained growth in Gross Domestic Product in the European Union.[37] Other success stories can be told about Viet Nam (which has not completely abandoned its planned economy), Poland, which has become one of the fastest growing economies in Europe, and so on and so forth. However, Cuba, only Cuba, is lagging behind. Why?

---

35 http://www.cuba.cu/gobierno/discursos/1989/esp/f260789e.html.

36 http://www.cuba.cu/gobierno/discursos/1991/esp/f161291e.html.

37 http://en.wikipedia.org/wiki/Economy_of_Slovakia.

PART II

THE WASTE

$$Chapter\ 5$$

ONE FIDEL PLAN FOR EACH PROVINCE AND THE ISLE OF PINES

I'm not a farm manager and that's not my work, but I'm interested in these problems and to
put my mind at ease I felt the need of undertaking a few little experiments ...
Fidel Castro.[1]

*O*f the dozens of projects that do not fall into the categories discussed in the following chapters, I have selected one for each province and the Isle of Pines for discussion in this chapter. Obviously, Fidel Castro believed in equal opportunity when distributing his agricultural expertise.

What were Fidel's Special Plans?

Castro's agricultural devotion started shortly after his arrival in Havana on January 8, 1959. Staying still with his bodyguards and other soldiers of his rebel Column, along with some administrative personnel, on the top floors of the Havana Hilton Hotel, he authorized the financing of what would become the first of his plans. Teresa Casuso, who was living with that group in the Havana Hilton, tells the following story: "One day, I was told, Fidel wrote out a check for $100,000 for a man who came to him with a project for planting rice in the Zapata swamp –a project which ended in total failure."[2] Castro himself announced the existence of that project on March 15, 1959 (see below).

---

1 Halperin (1992: 319).
2 (1961: 183).

Castro started conducting his "experiments" in the area of sugarcane production, that soon expanded into other fields and crops and livestock that started appearing throughout the island, with the name of "special plans" that were almost clandestine projects since no minister received a formal report and even sometimes were not aware of their existence.[3] These plans absorbed a great deal of Castro's time and energy, sometimes making him unavailable for days and weeks when important decisions had to be made.

Halperin wonders about how the financial aspects of his transactions were handled by the National Bank. Obviously, he did not get to find out that Fidel had a special account and managed the funds without ever giving a report. It was later known as "the account of the Commander in Chief.", or "the reserves of the Commander."[4]

Pinar del Río
San Andrés de Caiguanabo

Castro inaugurated this project on January 28, 1967.[5] According to him, besides the agricultural investment –mainly in coffee production— it also included a huge social investment.

The planning had taken place a year earlier. He announced the planting of one million coffee plants with a "new technique", meaning in terraces to avoid soil erosion. Castro also proclaimed the future use of other "modern techniques" such as "optimal fertilizer applications; and something else: the use of growth hormones." That was supposed to result in a harvest in less than a year.

Fidel Castro praised the people who worked on the project, building schools, houses, and sport centers. For him, the plan was of special importance: "This has much to do with the manner in which we want to build socialism and the manner in which we want to build communism." Castro was announcing to the world that Cuba was going to build socialism and communism simultaneously and had selected San Andrés de Caiguanabo as the first experimental site.

---

3 Halperin (1992: 320).

4 Álvarez (2008: 105-106) summarizes the testimonies of numerous sources about the origin and evolution of this banking activity.

5 http://www.cuba.cu/gobierno/discursos/1967/esp/f280167e.html.

His hope was that, with the social investment and the modern cultural techniques, coffee production in the project would increase three, four, even five times! The results obtained there would serve as a model for the rest of the country. It never happened. The plan failed. Today, the area shows the same appearance than the rest of the country: deteriorating social and agricultural investments, abandoned coffee plantations with none of the well-traced terraces with fast-growing coffee plants designed by Castro himself. The first communist community of the entire world is yet to come.

Despite the plan's failure, Fidel Castro awarded himself a luxurious residence and a farm located in the hills of San Andrés, where his coffee plants failed to produce.[6] Known as "the American's mansion", it was taken over by the State when the owner, Larry Lunt, went to prison in 1965, accused of being an agent of the Central Intelligence Agency of the United States.[7] The farm has over 1,325 acres and is devoted to livestock production. The majestic colonial-style mansion, surrounded by a wall and beautiful trees, has a nice swimming pool and a landing strip for the exclusive use of Fidel Castro.[8] The peasants of the area claim that the farm produces Cuba's most delicious cheeses.

---

6   Listed and described by CubaEuropa at http://www.cubaeuropa.com/historia/Fidel%20 Castro/Residencias.htm.

7   It was in that place that Ernesto Guevara and his men trained in 1966 for his Bolivian adventure (Castro and Ramonet 2006: 301).

8   The blog Cuba al Descubierto publishes a photo of Alexis Castro del Valle (one of Castro's sons) and his wife by the swimming pool of this house. More information at http://cubaaldescubierto.com/?p=4524.

As a final note, the inaugural ceremony of the project took place on the 114th anniversary of the birth of José Martí. Fidel did not mention Martí's name even once during his long speech. Exactly one year later, Fidel Castro would bring to trial the members of a group composed by militants of the Partido Socialista Popular, the political party that, before the triumph of the revolution, grouped the Marxist-Leninists of the country. Communism never arrived at San Andrés de Caiguanabo, but 37 of the old Cuban communists went to prison because of a purge instigated by Fidel, and the maximum leader added one more residence to the long list he had started right in the year he ascended into power.

La Habana
Oca Plan

"Operación Oca" or "Plan Oca del Comandante en Jefe," is a peculiar plan for two reasons: a strange creation and even a shorter duration.

Ocas are large tamed aquatic animals, very similar to geese, with white or gray feathers of different tones. They lay around 50 eggs per year, whose period of incubation is about 30 days. They get to live 20 years and can weigh more than 25 pounds. Ocas are primarily raised for their liver to make "foie gras" or *paté*, and also for their meat, eggs and feathers. They need plenty of space and enjoy foraging for their food. They are very productive and economical animals due a low maintenance cost.

How did this plan come about?[9] Chilean Max Marambio ("El guatón"),[10] a former bodyguard of Salvador Allende's, sought refuge in Cuba during the dictatorship of Augusto Pinochet, and became closely attached to Fidel Castro.

He arrived in Havana at the end of 1974, registered at the University of Havana and became a member of the Special Troops of the Ministry of Interior (MININT). In 1983, he brought to Cuba a sample of frozen *paté* from Paris that he shared in a dinner headed by Castro. The positive reaction to the delicacy was enough to start a business in partnership with Castro with 10 geese commandeered for the Havana Zoo. Only two survived but they were able to obtain 650 pounds of liver to prepare "foie gras". The Plan Oca was born!

---

9 See http://miguelpaz.blogspot.com/2004/03/reportaje-max-marambio.html.

10 //baracuteycubano.blogspot.com/2007/07/max-marambio.html.

The Castro-Marimbo business partnership operated from farms next to prison camps so the prisoners could provide free labor. Soon they were exporting products from more than one million geese in the form of feathers, meat and "foie gras". It became an important source of funds to finance MININT's secret operations. Despite the secret nature of the project, Fidel Castro mentioned it to get the unit's expanding into production of sheep and rabbits. [11]

The project ended as fast as it began. Today, the Cuban authorities are seeking Mr. Marambio for charges of bribery, fraud, embezzlement and forgery of bank documents.

This was not the first time Fidel Castro became involved in a project with small animals. Plans to breed goats were not successful in 1965.[12] In 1966, it was rabbits. A few years later, it was messenger pigeons, then, sheep, then, geese. Later, it was the big animals, namely buffaloes.

In a meeting of Party leaders, held on October 24, 1965, Castro promised:[13] "By 1970, we expect to produce 30,000,000 rabbits per year, which means that we can put a rabbit coat on every child if we want to, but we are not going to do this. It is better to export [the skins] to get a little money to enable us to carry out all these plans."

There are no goats, or rabbits or geese projects in Cuba today.

Matanzas
Zapata Swamp Plan

Interest in the Zapata Swamp[14] from U.S. companies was at its peak in the summer of 1912. Jenks documents "the marches and counter-marches [of the State

---

11   Speech of 7 March 1990 (http://www.cuba.cu/gobierno/discursos/1990/esp/f070390e.html).

12   In 2011, *Juventud Rebelde* announced the success of a similar plan started three years before in Las Villas http://www.juventudrebelde.cu/cuba/2011-03-26/crean-centros-de-reproduccion-animal-en-villa-clara/

13   http://lanic.utexas.edu/project/castro/db/1965/19651024-1.html.

14   The southern coast of Cuba west of Cienfuegos sprawls seaward in an enormous peninsula, shaped like a shoe –giving the name to it and to the swamp, which covers the greater part of its area.

Department] with respect to the Zapata land concession".[15] The efforts to acquire the area were full of contradictory reports about its worth. Despite the granting of a concession, the swamp was still in its pristine state when the revolution took power.

The swamp got Castro's immediate attention. As early as March 15, 1959, he declared: "… we are already studying and preparing the projects to desiccate the Zapata Swamp… 500,000 acres of land… when [that land] is ready for cultivation, is going to provide a livelihood to dozens of thousands Cuban families".[16] There were different ideas concerning the transformation of the Zapata Swamp since the early days of the revolution.[17] One important witness refers to the raising of crocodiles.[18] Dumont[19] recalls alerting Castro in August 1960 about the excessive cost of that project, stating that he did not want to see him obsessed with an irrelevant fantasy.

The project had started several months before. Newspapers showed photographs of Fidel Castro visiting the area and talking with the person in charge of

---

15 (1928: 107-110, 326).

16 Speech at the Central University "Marta Abreu" in Santa Clara, Las Villas, on March 15, 1959 (http://www.cuba.cu/gobierno/discursos/1959/esp/f150359e.html).

17 As stated above in this chapter, Casuso (1961: 483) documents Castro signing a check for $100,000 soon after victory for an American to start a project in the Zapata Swamp.

18 However, in his speech of January 15 of that year, Castro thanked Antonio Núñez Jiménez for convincing him to visit the Zapata Swamp and acknowledged that, because of his interest for, and knowledge of, that region, the government transformed the area into one of Cuba's most beautiful tourist destinations (http://www.cuba.cu/gobierno/discursos/1960/esp/f150160e.html).

19 (1971: 71).

the project, Commander William Morgan.[20] As in most cases, an announcement of the outcome of this project is yet to come.

Drying the swamp involved surrounding the area with dikes in order to avoid the flooding resulting from rains or the intrusion of marine waters. Once the soil looses the excessive humidity through drainage ditches it and can be cultivated. The crop selected was rice, whose cultivation is water-intensive. Dumont reacted: "I expect that this plan be preceded with a trip to Holland, where the Cubans will see how [the plan] is started with a pilot project".[21] The project ended as others.

Dumont, however, left Cuba before the Zapata Swamp project was extended to include another gigantic goal. Wotzkow[22] revealed that the original idea of *pedraplenes* (rock embankments used to connect nearby islands with the mainland) originated back in 1961 (the same time of Dumont's description). The plan consisted of building a highway-wall between Punta Mora (south of La Habana province) and Punta Gorda (in the western-most part of the Zapata Swamp), by filling the Ensenada de la Broa with garbage and soil removed from the western part of the country. The objective was to "enlarge" Cuba and drain the Zapata Swamp. The reasons for abandoning it included a plague of technical problems.

Today, the Zapata Swamp area is a tourism location with cabins for tourists. In addition, crocodile farms are providing raw material for an artisan industry that is also the source of needed foreign exchange.

Las Villas
Plan Banao

Banao is a small rural community located in the Escambray mountains, Sancti Spíritus municipality, Las Villas province. Because of its altitude and climate,

---

20 William Morgan was an American who fought with the guerrillas in the Sierra del Escambray in central Cuba during the struggle against Batista's dictatorship. He was one of the few Americans taking part in that struggle and the only one achieving the rank of Commander. After charging him with helping the new guerrillas fighting Castro's government in the Escambray, he lost his life in front of a firing squad in late 1961.

21 (1971: 170-171).

22 (1998: 138-139).

Fidel Castro decided to use this so-called "microclimate zone", as a testing ground for one of his agricultural plans.

On July 18, 1966, Castro announced to a group of students in Topes de Collantes –a sanatorium for patients with respiratory illnesses built in the 1950s— his plans for the area: 2,000 acres of grapevines and 665 acres of each strawberries, asparagus, onions and apples. Schools and day care centers would fulfill the needs of the large number of women who had enrolled in the program.[23]

On December 9 of that year,[24] during a speech in Santa Clara to more than 15,000 women, Castro made a startling revelation about the rapid progress of the Plan Banao: he intended to plant 670 acres that year because the 2.5-acre experimental plot had yielded over 30,000 pounds (12,000 lb/acre) of strawberries.

Because of Castro's tendency to exaggerate and to compete always for the first place, I decided to compare his figure with yields in other places. Randomly (the first entry provided by Google) I found a strawberry production guide published by the Extension Service at Penn State University.[25] It refers to strawberry yields in several states with a high degree of technology more than four decades after Castro's rudimentary experiment: "In the mid-Atlantic states,[26] a well-maintained matted-row strawberry planting of June bearers should produce an average of 10,000 pounds per acre, though yields range widely from half to twice this much."

Castro completed his revelation with the following announcement: the 30,000 pounds obtained from the experimental plot –along with the production obtained "from another plantation in Oriente" (he did not specified the place) had supplied the strawberries needed for the production of ice cream by the dairy industry, and to fulfill a series of demands." The plan in the Manzanillo area that did not produce enough strawberries to deserve a harvesting effort.[27]

---

23 http://www.cuba.cu/gobierno/discursos/1966/esp/f180766e.html.

24 During the V National Plenary of the Federation of Cuban Women (http://www.cuba.cu/gobierno/discursos/1966/esp/f091266e.html).

25 http://extension.psu.edu/business/ag-alternatives/horticulture/fruits/strawberry-production.

26 The mid-Atlantic states include Delaware, Maryland, New Jersey, New York, North Carolina, Pennsylvania and Virginia.

27 Personal communication at that time with a person working in the Fruits and Vegetables Enterprise.

Let us discuss the veracity of the statement concerning the production of strawberries in a 2.5-acre plot satisfying the country's demand for strawberry ice cream. On June 4, 1966, the Cuban regime opened the Coppelia ice cream parlor in the Vedado area of Havana. Soon many more followed in the rest of the island. Two factors contributed to the popularity of Coppelia: the fact that ice cream was not available elsewhere and the excellent quality of the 26 flavors and 25 combinations. People were willing to stand in line for several hours to consume the famous ice creams. At the time of Castro's speech, Coppelia served 4,250 gallons of ice cream to 35,000 customers each day.[28] Using the ratio of 1 pound of (hulled, with the leafy stem removed) strawberries per 16 portions of ice cream,[29] the 30,000 pounds of strawberries produced in the pilot plot would have served 480,000 customers. Since Coppelia's inauguration, the business served 35,000 customers a day or 12,775,000 per year (365 days). If we knew how many of the 12.8 million customers consumed strawberry ice cream, we could deduct 480,000 from that number to measure the size of Fidel Castro's lie.

His enthusiasm for the alleged success of the strawberry experiment led Castro to announce that the following year they would be planting 270 times more strawberries. However, there was a problem. As reported by Dumont, the strawberries grew in the best-drained slopes, with around 1 kg of fertilizer used every square foot and completely concentrated on the buds. The result: they burned in with the first rain.

Almost forty-four years later, the newspaper *Juventud Rebelde*, in its edition of August 20, 2010,[30] published a long report remembering Castro's speech of 1966. Titled "The revolution of women"; it contains interviews with three women who were present at the 1966 speech. It happens that Banao set the pace for the incorporation of women in the work force and their advancement. Banao would have been impossible without the participation of thousands of women. One of them declared, "More than a utopia, Banao was the proof of what women were capable of doing."

---

28 http://en.wikipedia.org/wiki/Coppelia_%28ice_cream_parlor%29.

29 http://thepioneerwoman.com/cooking/2013/07/strawberry-ice-cream/

30 http://www.juventudrebelde.cu/cuba/2010-08-20/la-revolucion-de-las-mujeres-/

The utopia was the Plan Banao itself! There is not one word about the unrealized output of thousands of pounds of onions, asparagus, strawberries and all other exotic crops. Today, Banao is a tourist place. Needless to say, Coppelia could not survive without the supply of strawberries from the plan and today most of the parlors are closed and, those open, offer no more than a couple of flavors of a very poor quality.

Camagüey
The IR-8 Rice Project

The "green revolution" is a term that refers to the significant increase in agricultural productivity resulting from the introduction of high-yield varieties of grains, the use of fertilizer, pesticides, irrigation, and improved management techniques that took place between the 1940s and the late 1960s, mainly in the latter years. For better implementation, a network of agricultural research centers was established: the Consultative Group on International Agricultural Research (CGIAR). It was developed by the World Bank and supported by international organizations such as FAO. The net benefits of such production increases are the subject of a debate. Some argue about high energy consumption; others consider the bottlenecks represented by lack of transportation and other impediments in developing countries.

The IR-8 was a semi-dwarf rice variety developed by the International Rice Research Institute (IRRI) in the Philippines. Since it could produce more grain per plant when grown with certain fertilizers and irrigation –almost 10 times in some cases—it was called the "miracle rice". Right after the results of the experiments reported by De Datta in 1968, Fidel Castro saw in that variety an excellent opportunity to increase rice production and immediately developed a plan in the province of Camagüey.

The project to establish rice paddies using the IR-8 rice cultivar was a relative success, but there was a problem. According to Dumont,[31] about 1,087 acres in the southern plains of Camagüey were prepared for rice seed production. To finish the job, a drainage ditch was needed but it was not built before June's strong rains and,

---

31 (1971: 170).

as a result, the heavily seeded acreage was covered by one meter of water and the rice rotted. To reproduce the new rice seeds faster, an expert recommended placing the seedbeds under plastic arcs. Castro mobilized 200 volunteers for a month to build by hand 15 acres of rice paddies on terraces over rolling hills, despite so many plains in Cuba. Wrongly interpreting the technician's advice, Fidel wanted to speed up the rice growth by placing, on posts four meters tall, three thousand huge lamps, similar to those used in circuses to provide continuous heat. Dumont points out that he forgot that hot air ascends and that the excessive use of light slows the ripening of certain rice varieties. No one on his technical team dared to point out his mistake neither to suggest taking advantage of the opportunity to start a circus with the lamps, the clown and the clapping audience.

The following year, on October 18, 1969, Castro announced that 232,120 acres of the miracle rice were under production.[32] He intended to plant about 132,640 more at the end of the year and to double that in the following spring.

The official press continued reporting the successes on rice production. However, rice is still under the rationing system and the country imports about 500,000 pounds of rice per year, which is close to total consumption requirements.

Oriente
Vegetable Gardens in Mayarí Pinewoods

Fidel Castro fell in love with that area at an early age. He would ride a horse from Birán taking the riskier way to enjoy the solitude and beauty of the top of the mountains (see chapter 2). For that reason, there is no mystery in his efforts to develop plans for the area.

The first question that comes to mind is, "why look for places like Pinares de Mayarí when there are so many uncultivated plains close to urban centers?" The answer is Castro's constant search for spectacular and out of the ordinary projects. That was his challenge! Let us read how he described this place to the

---

32 Commencement ceremony of students of Agronomy and technicians of the Agricultural Technological Institutes, held in the Central University of Las Villas, Santa Clara, http://www.cuba.cu/gobierno/discursos/1969/esp/f181069e.html.

people he encountered on their way to the II Eastern Front "Frank País" on September 26, 1966.[33]

The half-million inhabitants of the area faced the following inconveniences: lack of communications; low labor productivity because machinery was not available; the prevalence of *minifundia;* soil erosion because farming was done without regards for the steep slopes, that sometimes reach 80 or 90 degrees, which renders the soil poor after two or three crop cycles; and total absence of fertilization.

Mining and slash and burn agriculture had turned the area into almost a desert. There was a need to change that situation. Castro believed that technology could return the soil productivity. For example, recognizing that it was impossible to get heavy machinery such as bulldozers and tractors to the area, he proposed the use of some types of portable machines, like lawn mowers. Although pushed by hand, they are better than the hoe and the machete.

Castro started with a reforestation program intending to plant thousands of pine trees. Wondering why those soils were so unproductive, he decided to do some testing. He dropped a few tons or organic matter and fertilizer in a few acres and obtained unbelievable results. The corn grew, and grew well. A second round of experiments included 20 acres with 10 parcels and the results were surprising: the one and a half acre of melons produced 6,800 pounds (around 1,200 melons). The tomato, onion and pepper parcels rendered good quality and relative good yield. Therefore, he made plans for the following year. He would plant 5,000 acres of vegetables, which would be rotated with legumes, maybe alfalfa. He was planning on 2,000 cows in stables that would produce at least 10,000 liters of milk per day. The idea of building cowsheds in a mountainous area with 70-80° slope was probably anticipating the massive protest of the 2,000 cows that would refuse to graze there unless safely tied to a solid pine tree with a reinforced rope. Castro had probably read *Animal farm* and was trying to avoid another "Battle of the Cowshed".[34] In addition, how were the milkmen going to do their job under such conditions?

---

33 http://www.cuba.cu/gobierno/discursos/1966/esp/f260966e.html.
34 Orwell (1991: 124).

He also announced that they were extracting 100,000 tons of filter mud, manure and other organic matters. Castro ordered 150 trucks constantly going up with organic matter (50 of them with lime because the pH in this area is a low 5.5). Of course, there would be the need of yearly applications and jobs for 500 technicians from the second year of middle school.

The excitement produced by the experimental results did not allow Castro to realize that his plan rested on ferrous lands. According to Dumont, the soil is too filtering, subject to erosion and unfeasible for vegetable production. Castro grew legumes there successfully on an alluvium bottom after taking thousands of truckloads of soil, dozens of kilometers of pipes, building beautiful stables, but there was no forage. However, he never stopped praising the project.

During the meeting with the Delegates selected to attend the IX Festival of the Youth and Students on June 26, 1965, Fidel Castro stated that he thought that in lieu of the Algeria's suspended festival the delegates should go to Mayari Pinewoods to perform voluntary work.[35] He told the Delegates that planting one million pine trees would be a modest contribution to that project. There was ample supply of small trees.

On May 18, 1967, he spoke again about it.[36] He claimed to have started production on the lateritic, red soils of the Pinewoods, where only pines grew

---

35 http://www.cuba.cu/gobierno/discursos/1965/esp/f260665e.html.
36 Closing ceremony of the III National Congress of ANAP, on 18 of May 1967. His speech can be found at http://www.cuba.cu/gobierno/discursos/1967/esp/f180567e.html.

before. He discouraged farmers who were planting *viandas* and plantains. The regime was planting forest trees. A few days later,[37] he congratulated the Italian technicians who were turning arid soils into damns in the same project, making the soils absorb much more water to increase productivity up to 50%. The project ended a few months later. The beauty of the area was the driving force behind the building of a few motels that cater to tourists during the entire year.

Fidel Castro himself is also a guest at least once a year... but in his own mansion located behind a hill called "La Mensura", close to his parents' estate in Mayarí Pinewoods.[38] He used it to rest after hunting in a nearby area called "La Melba". Selected personnel take care of the place and the desires of the Cuban ex-President serving him during his annual visits.

Isle of Pines
A Citrus Plan, Communism and a New Man

To build communism, simultaneously with the material base, a new man must be created.
Ernesto (Che) Guevara.[39]

---

37 At ANAP's bean festival in Velazco, Oriente, on 16 June 1967: http://www.cuba.cu/gobierno/discursos/1967/esp/f160667e.html.

38 http://www.cubaeuropa.com/historia/Fidel%20Castro/Residencias.htm. See also http://www.desdecuba.com/mason/?p=6379.

39 "Socialism and the man in Cuba". Letter to Carlos Quijano, editor of Uruguay's *Marcha,* who published this letter on 12 March 1965 (http://www.marxists.org/espanol/guevara/65-socyh.htm).

Fidel Castro's Agricultural Follies

Why not aspire to convert also the region [of the Isle of Pines]
in the first communist region of Cuba?
Fidel Castro.[40]

Introduction

Since the early days of the revolution, the Isle of Pines (an 850-square mile island located 30 miles south of Cuba, across the Gulf of Batabanó) showed potential for agricultural and social development.[41] In 1961, Castro announced the creation of a fruit trees plan that commenced the following year with the planting of 2,000 acres with the guidance of Soviet advisors and a completion date of 1966. In 1964, the President of the National Institute of Agrarian Reform (INRA) Carlos Rafael Rodríguez visited the area and approved the goal of planting 20,000 acres by 1966. However, Fidel Castro "adjusted" the plan two years later after deciding that the plan should include around 1,650 acres of pineapple and papaya and no less than 330 acres of fruit plantains. Hurricane Alma hit the Isle of Pines on June 6, 1966 causing severe damages to this and other agricultural endeavors.

The Agricultural Prospective Plan

A new specific plan for the Isle of Pines became public in December 1967, after the establishment by Fidel Castro of a set of directives for the economic and social development of the region. This plan, that would cover the period 1968-1980, counted with the massive labor provided by the Agricultural Youth Columns, some of which remained permanently on the island. Also included was the building of cold storage and processing plants. To carry out the project, hundreds of youth continued to arrive, some for a 2-month period, some for longer stays. At the end of the mobilization, there were 1,100 youngsters working between 12 and 13 hours daily. In the 1970s, there was also an increase in the arrival of young students —organized under the system of the middle and high

---

40   Speech in the Isle of Pines on 12 August 1967 (http://www.cuba.cu/gobierno/discursos/1967/esp/f120867e.html).

41   The information until the end of this section and the entire next section is based on EcuRed (http://www.ecured.cu/index.php/Isla_de_la_Juventud_%28Agricultura%29).

schools in the countryside —to work mainly on the citrus plan. Castro himself declared that, at some point in time, there would be 40,000 young students on the island.[42]

The plan was ambitious indeed. To the original citrus and other fruits, Castro added other commodities and tasks, including dams and reservoirs, roads and highways. Agricultural diversification included large extensions of beans, pigeon peas, tubers and roots, pumpkin, vegetables, melons, tomatoes, coffee, and many others.

The Isle of Youth is Born

As part of "the process of institutionalization", started in 1976, the political and administrative divisions of the country were changed. The Isle of Pines was renamed the Isle of Youth and became a Special Municipality in 1978.

The Ideological Dimension

In Castro's mind, the conditions appeared favorable for the testing of a startling innovation. Several factors combined to give him a revisionist idea. The isolation of the Isle of Youth, the thousands and thousands of students and young people by then living permanently there, offered an objective scenario. Guevara's obsession with the creation of a new man, and Fidel Castro's systematic *modus operandi* of deviating from the norm, contributed the subjective conditions. Fidel Castro believed that the Isle of Youth was fertile ground for building socialism and communism simultaneously. Apparently, he had forgotten that, in January 28 of that year –a little over six months before—, he had proclaimed San Andrés de Caiguanabo in Pinar del Río province, as the first experimental communist region of Cuba. He was now assigning that role to the Isle of Youth, which he intended to convert into the first communist region of the world! "What kind of life do you believe should be the life of the men and women in this region of the country? Why do not we turn this area into the first communist region of Cuba? Let us also put our minds … to resolve as the vanguard of our people, the problems involved in the idea of creating a communist society."[43]

---

42 http://www.cuba.cu/gobierno/discursos/1975/esp/f200675e.html.
43 Speech in the Isle of Pines on 12 August 1967. (http://www.cuba.cu/gobierno/discursos/1967/esp/f120867e.html).

Evaluation

Production

A Report issued by FAO[44] in 2003 states that Cuba's Citrus National Program fulfilled expectations. For example, citrus production since 1975 grew at an annual average rate of 14%. It reached over one million tons in 1990 in an area of 115,000 ha. Citrus became one of the most important export commodities, with annual income of US$ 180 million. However, the sudden disappearance of the socialist bloc brought about great losses to Cuba's citrus industry. By 1994, production had declined by one-half. On August 30, 2008, hurricane Gustav damaged citrus groves and processing facilities in the Isle of Youth, as well as housing, industrial facilities and the main hospital.

The truth of the matter is that, besides the disappearance of the subsidies from the Soviet Union, and the damage inflicted by hurricanes, the main culprit for the disaster of the citrus plan was the huanglongbing (HLB), a devastating insect that affects citrus. Cuba had reported the existence of HLB to the Citrus Interamerican Network and the FAO in 2007. The expert technicians praised by Castro so many times, failed to anticipate this plague and acquire the knowledge and the means to combat it. Interestingly enough, the mentioned article,[45] recognizes "today's new strategy involves the implementation of an efficient technology for the management of plagues and bioinsurance", trying to rescue the crop although to a lesser degree.

What is unbelievable, when compared to the figures mentioned by Castro at the beginning of the project, is that the recovery plan aims at planting only 2,000 ha by the year 2020, reporting that in June 2013, only 22 of the 175 ha programmed for 2013 had been realized. An interesting remark appears in the article: "When citrus disappeared from the local economic plans, its culture also crumbled; however, it is necessary to revive it". Later statements about nurseries

---

44 http://www.fao.org/docrep/meeting/006/y9316s.htm#P20_723.

45 "Requiem por el "naranjo del patio"" in *Juventud Rebelde,* 18 June 2013. (http://www.juventudrebelde.cu/cuba/2013-06-18/requiem-por-el-naranjo-del-patio/).

and plantations, however, sound more like bad management[46] and abandonment of the plan than the previous insect damage reported.

I agree with the group of qualified people[47] who argue that the excuses given by the Cuban regime to justify the failure of the citrus plan are not valid by any stretch of the imagination. To accept them we would need a solid explanation of why none of the citrus-producing countries in tropical and template zones lost their industries for the same reasons. The bottom line is that, without the huge soviet subsidies, even with a decent flow of foreign capital, the Cuban citrus industry was unable to survive.

Building Communism

The revisionist idea of building socialism and communism simultaneously in one region of the country failed drastically. The disaster of the 1970 sugar campaign forced Castro to return under Soviet tutelage and the revisionist project had to be let go. Cuba returned to Soviet-style socialism.

The New Man

The creation of a new man was not only Guevara's dream, as most people tend to believe. During his speech of July 26, 1968,[48] Fidel Castro emphasized that the great task of the revolution was "the creation of a new man, a man with true revolutionary conscience".

According to Montaner,[49] "Che wanted to multiply himself. He tried —perhaps unconsciously—to impregnate millions of Cubans with his seed…To the plump little man who goes and returns to work, to the husband bureaucrat in the municipality, to the man who sings in the shower, Guevara was asking for the moon." The new man dreamt by Guevara and Castro is yet to be born in Cuba.

---

46 See "El citrico cubano aspira a crecer a partir de 2013", *Juventud Rebelde*", 22 June 2008. (http://www.juventudrebelde.cu/cuba/2008-06-22/el-citrico-cubano-aspira-crecer-a-partir-del-2013/).

47 See, for example, the article by Roberto Álvarez-Quinones entitled "Cuba: ¿Y los cítricos qué… sueño que se derrumbó", AOL Noticias, 19 August 2011. (http://noticias.aollatino.com/2011/08/19/cuba-citricos/).

48 http://www.cuba.cu/gobierno/discursos/1968/esp/f260768e.html

49 (1994: 121, 122).

After decades of sacrifices, lack of opportunities for advancement and with no hope in sight, the Cuban youth have been leaving the country by the thousands. Corruption is rampant in every activity and the social fabric of the country is farther than ever from the creation of that new man.

It could not be otherwise. In April 1967, during the development of the plans for the Isle of Youth, Ernesto Guevara sent his famous "Message to the Tricontinental"[50] an international gathering in the Cuban capital. Allow me to quote just a few sentences:

> ... Hatred as an element of the struggle; a relentless hatred of the enemy, impelling us over and beyond the natural limitations that man is heir to and transforming him into an effective, violent, selective and cold killing machine. Our soldiers must be thus; a people without hatred cannot vanquish a brutal enemy.

To anybody's standards, that is not the way to create a new man.

---

50 http://www.marxists.org/archive/guevara/1967/04/16.htm.

Chapter 6

THE OBSESSION WITH LABOR MOBILIZATIONS

[Our goal is that] women, soldiers, students, an entire human swarm,
with all of the country's resources, turn towards agricultural production,
turn towards all plantings along and across the country.
Fidel Castro.[1]

Since the early years of the revolution, free time in Cuba has had a social value, used in the ideological and economic areas for the national reconstruction,[2] and considered of utmost importance in the development of the "new man". Who performs voluntary work?: (a) employed workers outside the ordinary labor force; (b) unemployed women; (c) students during the school year or vacations; (d) prisoners; and (e) military draft recruits.[3]

Early Mobilizations

"Volunteers" worked in a disorganized manner in the early times of the revolution performing productive work (*trabajo productivo*). Despite the obvious advantages

---

1 Speech at the V National Plenary of the Federation of Cuban Women at the Sandino Stadium, Santa Clara, December 9, 1966 (http://www.cuba.cu/gobierno/discursos/1966/esp/f091266e. html).

2 Statement by Antonio Núñez Jiménez at UNESCO's 1966 International Seminar on Free Time and Recreation (Mesa-Lago 1973: 679).

3 Mesa-Lago (1973:682).

of guaranteed labor supply and free cost, the overall expenses must have been extremely high.[4]

The number of people involved was always high and grew significantly during some time periods. For example, statistics gathered for 1967 on the number of person-years of voluntary work were as follows:[5] 60,000 to 70,000 employed workers; 5,000 to 10,000 unemployed women; 20,000 to 27,000 middle school and university students; 84,000 to 120,000 military recruits; and 20,000 to 75,000 prisoners. The economic benefit of this free labor force is twofold. Firstly, they provide workers when regular labor is not available. Secondly, they save wages and salaries, which ranged from 16 million pesos in 1962 to 97.8 million pesos in 1967.

The disadvantages, however, appear to outweigh the monetary savings. To mention just a few:[6] 1. Low productivity. 2. Damage to future harvests in perennial crops, such as coffee, as inexperienced students harvested green grains by "milking" the branches. 3. Increase in labor accidents. 4. Less classroom hours. 5. Cost of transportation, housing and other expenses.

Although recognizing the following experience to be an extreme case, Medea Benjamin and co-authors[7] describe a Sunday outing to pick up potatoes in Havana's countryside. The volunteers waited from six to 8 a.m. until the bus arrived; the driver then circled around for two hours before finding the farm. When, after the snack, they were ready to start working, they typically faced three possibilities: 1. they were in the wrong place; 2. they were in the right place but the field was already harvested; or 3. the farm was the right one and the potatoes were waiting for the volunteers, but there was no one available to guide and organize them. After wondering around for a while, they returned to the bus at noon because the farm was not supposed to provide lunch for them. The return trip would be full of jokes and the repeated phrase "You'd think that after all

---

4 Dumont (1971: 102-104) contains several descriptions of these early weekly mobilizations with their inefficiencies and low productivity. Fagen (1969) also discusses them more in depth.

5 Mesa-Lago (1973: 689).

6 Mesa-Lago (1973: 700-708).

7 Benjamin et al. (1985: 185).

these years…" Benjamin et al recognized that "the overall productivity of such labor was so low that by the late 1970s, such Sunday outings were eliminated."

Throughout the years, Castro developed countless forms of mobilizing labor to work in different tasks. Time and experience were useful in devising ways to keep Cubans under control in permanent agricultural projects. New names, drawn from military organizations, became part of the revolutionary jargon: Unit, Column, Brigade, Contingent, Battalion, and many others. Their numbers grew exponentially. For example, in a speech of May 31, 1970,[8] Castro mentioned that, for an area near the city of Bayamo, 40 brigades were not enough, and that the following year there would be 30 heavy brigades and many more drainage brigades, dam brigades, irrigation brigades, plus 20 construction brigades. He was referring to just an area in one province. The following sections contain examples of permanent labor mobilizations.

The Military Units to Help Production (U.M.A.P.)

For the purpose of this book, the *Unidades Militares de Ayuda a la Producción* (UMAP) represented a huge agricultural fiasco. For the recruits and their families they convey a painful human tragedy.[9] Fidel Castro himself conceived them, giving an early hint during his speech of March 13, 1963,[10] when he stated that some people had the wrong attitude towards the revolution and that there was a need of agricultural labor. The proletarians, he added, have hard hands to deal with that problem. The government was already building camps in the plains of Camagüey province to put those citizens to work.

On November 9, 1965, the Cuban government started gathering young people from around the country and sending them permanently to UMAP camps. The "recruits" who did not show up in the place and time on their citations to join the

---

8 Speech during the inauguration of the new town in Doce y Medio for the workers of the Rice Plan, Bayamo, Oriente, May 31, 1970 (http://www.cuba.cu/gobierno/discursos/1970/esp/f310570e. html).

9 Parts of this section are based on personal recollections and the account of Emelina Núñez-Prado entitled "U.M.A.P.: Where there was never a human gesture" sent to me by electronic mail. Those interested can consult Ronet (1987), Viera (2002), Castro Figueroa (2011: 55-64) or Cabrera (2012).

10 http://www.cuba.cu/gobierno/discursos/1963/esp/f130363e.html

UMAP, were picked up by uniformed officials at their homes, the streets of their neighborhoods, their schools and churches, or at popular gathering places. They were transported by trains, buses and trucks, guarded by members of the Ministry of the Interior (MININT) bearing semi-automatic weapons, to the province of Camagüey and divided into groups of about 120. In total, about 25,000 people went through the UMAP, which lasted for more than two-and-a-half- years, until July 1968.

Their destinations were several sugar mills. Barbed wire fencing with one entry and exit gate surrounded the buildings that housed them. There was also one sentry post with a permanent guard carrying loaded weapons. The recruits had to endure forced labor, insults, humiliations, and beatings. They were obviously prisoners; the name "recruits" pretended to equate them with the real recruits of the draft (*servicio militar obligatorio*, SMO).

There were eight central units called "agrupación" [grouping], known by the name of the city nearby their location: Chambas, Ciego de Ávila, Esmeralda, Nuevitas, Vertientes, Camagüey, Florida and Morón. Each grouping had five (sometimes, more) battalions; each battalion had four companies and each of the latter had three or four platoons of 150 men each. (Thus, 150 x 4 x 5 x 8 = 24,000). In the autumn of 1966, considered the point of peak enrollment, the figure reached 25,000 people.

They worked in the agricultural fields from sunrise to sunset. Although very few had any agricultural experience, they had to perform every task in sugarcane production.

International pressure led to the dismantling of the UMAPs, which resulted in a huge agricultural fiasco. Despite the free labor, costs must have run in the millions of pesos.

After July 1968, other names replaced UMAP. The following group was the first one and, not coincidentally, occupied its housing units.

The Nameless Brigades: "Earning" the Right to Leave the Country

Fidel Castro was also the creator of the agricultural labor brigades that replaced the UMAPs. Castro referred to them during his speech of September 28, 1968: "Those who opted for the Yankee "dolce vita" and obtained their documents and their passports have also to participate in the people's effort, because they cannot live as parasites. While they wait for the little telegram [with the authorization to leave the country], the Johnsons… are earning their bread by the sweat of their brows."[11]

Unlike the UMAPs, these brigades were not "baptized". Castro referred to their members as "the Johnsons", after U.S. President Lyndon B. Johnson, in office at that time. He did not mention the destination of these thousands of men sent to agricultural camps far away from their homes.

The organization was similar to the UMAPs, but the treatment was not that severe. Internees worked several hours, mainly in sugarcane cultural activities, for an undetermined period of time that could extend for several years.

The closing of this project, after the disaster of the 1970 sugar campaign, added another failure to an already long list of Castro's agricultural initiatives. It is impossible to calculate the cost and the number of people involved.

The Centennial Youth Column (CJC)

Fidel Castro had another idea to organize labor brigades mainly composed by young people. The Centennial Youth Column, born in 1968 and in existence for three years, was created for young workers. At one point, it reached 24,000 members, working mainly in Camagüey province's sugarcane activities. Castro praised them saying that it was the most productive force in the 1970 sugar campaign, and 73 of its members were recognized as national work heroes.[12]

A foreign observer stated, "the Centennial Youth Column was one of Castro's astute political maneuvers, sending many thousands of working-class youth to study trades, cut cane, and clear lands in Camagüey Province, a naturally rich but under populated and traditionally conservative area".[13] The merging of the CJC with other production brigades gave birth to the Work Youth Army (Ejército Juvenil del Trabajo -EJT).

---

11 http://www.cuba.cu/gobierno/discursos/1968/esp/f280968e.html.
12 Speech of 4 April 1972, during the closing of the II Congress of the UJC (http://www.cuba.cu/ gobierno/discursos/1972/esp/f040472e.html).
13 Gall (1971: 55).

The Work Youth Army (EJT)

It was created on August 3, 1973, with the fusion of the Centennial Youth Column and the permanent Infantry Divisions of the Revolutionary Armed Forces. Oftentimes called "a combatant and productive force" the EJT is part of the ground forces of the Revolutionary Armed Forces (FAR), and had the following mission:[14]

- To conduct productive activities aimed at the socio-economic development of the country.
- To implement measures to protect the environment and the rational use of natural resources.
- To give military training to its members, allowing them to participate in the armed struggle.
- To contribute to the education and development of the youth with respect to patriotism, military, work, and sports.

Its structure consists of divisions, regiments and battalions. Its members receive their salaries and wages of the job they perform, like the rest of the country's workers. The Cuban press is constantly reporting about their productive performance in the agricultural sector. This appears to be the only remaining mass mobilization mechanism of the youth performing agricultural productive activities under military discipline.

The Production and Defense Brigades

Law-Decree No. 72 of August 9, 1983, established the Territorial Militia Troops (MTT) in an atmosphere of military conflict that developed in Cuba during the Reagan Administration. The "war of all the people" went beyond the military preparedness for an "imminent" U.S. invasion, also working in the preservation of food supplies under war conditions. The Production and Defense Brigades were a parallel organization to the MTTs; they were composed of non-military volunteers. Their numbers reached over three million members in more than 60,000 Brigades.[15]

---

14   http://www.cubagob.cu/otras_info/minfar/far/ejt.htm.

15   http://www.cubagob.cu/otras_info/minfar/doctrina/bpd.htm.

Students in Agriculture

It would be almost impossible to find a person who does not support a country's investment in human capital. That issue is out of the scope of this section. The efforts of the Cuban educational system have paid off with an educated population and a highly qualified labor force. Very few would question that achievement. Combining studies with work is also a healthy practice. The issue at hand is the way school and work were combined in Cuba for secondary and high school students during 40 years. There was no need to send the student population to live and work in rural areas full-time when other alternatives were available. This section deals with the moral and physical damage of such practices along with their high cost of that project that also came out of Fidel Castro's mind.

The Ideological Motivation and the Ulterior Motive

Combining schooling with work —especially in agriculture due to the labor scarcity— was one of Castro's early goals of his reform of the educational system.[16] Since education was an integral part of the building of a socialist society, the school-work link also had a moral and an ideological justification: the creation of a new man and closing the gap between the city and the countryside.[17]

There was also an ulterior motive recognized by foreign scholars and Fidel Castro himself. Gasperini believes that, at least at the beginning, another goal was that "the entire cost of the education system was to be covered by the students' productive labor"[18] Fidel Castro maintained that goal during his tenure in power.

In early January 1971, Castro stated his intention of adding, within a ten-year period, "700,000 young people to economic activity [with] those in middle education, in technological institutes... and university students; that is, those in

---

16 Lutjens (1998) contains a selected annotated bibliography of books and articles dealing with the issue of education in socialist Cuba. Other interesting pieces include Figueroa et al. (1974), Carnoy (1981), McGuire and Vocke (1988), and the international perspective of Arenas et al. (2006).

17 For a discussion about the moral education in a revolutionary society (examples used include China, Cuba and Tanzania), see Ruscoe (1975). Barkin (1980) discusses the issue of the separation of town and country.

18 Gasperini (2000: 17).

higher education, starting in their third year would be enrolled in production plans".[19] During the inaugural ceremony of a Secondary School in the country-side on April 25,1971,[20] he referred to the fact that the agricultural production "would cover the investment costs and the expenses of these schools." He added that, if that was the case, an unlimited number of those schools could be built. A couple of months later, speaking at another school inauguration,[21] Castro went beyond the previous statement: "So from the economic point of view, produc-tion would exceed by far the value of investments and the annual cost of these schools."

Two years later, he reiterated the importance of both goals: "This reflects the importance of study and work, the need to continue developing the idea to introduce the students to production, so that one day our school system becomes essentially financed by the students' work".[22] There goes the myth of free education!

The Beginning and End of Student Mobilizations

On July 24, 2011, the newspaper *Juventud Rebelde* made a surprising announce-ment, reproduced in all national and some foreign media: the demise of the voluntary work performed in student mobilizations. By itself, the decision made by President Raúl Castro should not be a surprise since the country is experienc-ing a very difficult economic situation. The surprise was the revelation that the practice –introduced by Ernesto Guevara at the beginning of the revolution[23]— had evolved into "gigantic mobilizations to agricultural fields or other activities, without a productive component, where waste of time was rampant and waste

---

19 Speech at the inauguration of a middle school in Ceiba, January 7, 1971 (http://www.cuba.cu/ gobierno/discursos/1971/esp/f070171e.html).

20 http://www.cuba.cu/gobierno/discursos/1971/esp/f250471e.html.

21 In the inauguration of the Basic Secondary School in the Countryside built in the Isle of Pines, on 29 June 1971 (http://www.cuba.cu/gobierno/discursos/1971/esp/f290671e.html).

22 Speech at the inauguration of numerous school buildings for the 1973-74 school year held at the Technological Institute of Electronics "Eduardo García Delgado" in Boyeros, La Habana, October 22, 1973 (http://www.cuba.cu/gobierno/discursos/1973/esp/f221073e.html).

23 For a detailed description of the steps taken in 1959 in that direction, see http://www.bohe-mia.cu/2009/10/08/historia/trabajo-voluntario.html.

of resources was far higher than the economic impact of the work realized." [24]
In the future, people would perform voluntary work in cases of natural disasters
and other events that resulted in damage to agricultural production or some services. After reading the previous announcement, the early phases of this type of
revolutionary event come to mind.

In 1962, tens of thousands of boarding students were sent to the mountains
of Oriente province to harvest coffee. That was the beginning of a systematic
program whereas middle-school students would perform productive industrial
or agricultural tasks, which could encompass a weekend, a vacation period or
whatever time it took to respond to urgent production needs. Two years later, on
May 1964, the Ministry of Education issued Resolution No. 392 linking physical and intellectual work through three types of activities: instruction, productive and social works.[25] Almost a year later, Fidel Castro stated that the week of
homage to Giron heroes would coincided with the traditional recess of the Holy
Week.[26]

The School to the Countryside

The first experience with the "school to the countryside" took place from April
23 to May 29, 1966 —one year after Castro's announcement, when students and
personnel of the middle and high schools arrived in people's farms in Camagüey
province. The group consisted of 7,000 students from that province and 10,000
from boarding schools in Havana. The practice continued every year and became
part of the school calendar for all middle schools of the country.[27]

The "school **to** the countryside" (*escuela al campo*) —defining the students' systematic and organized participation in productive tasks— served as a transition to
what later became "school **in** the countryside" (*escuela en el campo*).

---

24 This was the reaction of the newspaper *Trabajadores* (http://www.oem.com.mx/laprensa/
notas/n2169541.htm).

25 Figueroa et al. (1974: 13-14).

26 Speech in the ceremony celebrating the fourth anniversary of the victory in Playa Giron,
Havana, April 19, 1965 (http://www.cuba.cu/gobierno/discursos/1965/esp/f190465e.html).

27 Figueroa et al. (1974: 14).

The School in the Countryside

The system started in the 1968-1969 school year with "secondary school", covering the 7th through 9th grades. The students lived in rural settings, attended classes and performed agricultural tasks, keeping their ties with their families through passes to visit their homes during weekends.[28]

A uniform compound with a total building area of around 7,000 square meters on 1,320 acres was intended to serve 500 boarding students.[29]

At the end of 1973, Fidel Castro informed that the system of study and work consisted of middle schools in the countryside, polytechnic institutes, and universities; there were 140,000 students in the study-work system that were tending to 182,380 acres of various crops. One-hundred and two schools, mostly for boarding students, had been built; 65 were middle schools in the countryside and a few –in a trial test– were high schools in the countryside.[30]

Evaluation

Evaluation of productive work conducted through voluntary mobilizations in the early years of the revolution appears in Dumont.[31] In addition to the slovenliness and excessive production costs per unit, he found that the productivity of most volunteers was not even one-fourth of agricultural workers' productivity. Dumont based his conclusion on the fact that an efficient sugarcane cutter would cut 3.5 to 4 tons per day, with a maximum of 7 tons. Students of agricultural schools who had some experience would cut between 1.5 to 8 tons; other adolescents less than 1 ton; the best cutters among volunteer citizens, 500 kg; the rest, between 250 and 300 kg. It is obvious that bureaucrats and intellectual workers are not prepared to perform that type of physical work.

Similar examples existed in coffee, vegetables, fruits, ornamentals, and other agricultural crops. In the case of the school in the countryside, to the productive

---

28 Figueroa et al. (1974: 14, 15).

29 Figueroa et al. (1974: 46) refers to 6,959.25 m², while in an anonymous publication the figure of 7,700 m² is mentioned (Secundaria Basica Rural Tipica, n.d., p. 39).

30 Speech of October 22, 1973 (http://www.cuba.cu/gobierno/discursos/1973/esp/f221073e.html).

31 (1971: 102-104).

parameters one would need to add the reduction in the time devoted to academic activities. Despite being so obvious, Castro stated the opposite in a speech on January 30, 1967 when he was organizing this new effort.[32] After saying that the idea was to divide the time between schooling (50%), productive work (30%) and physical education and sports activities (20%), he exclaimed, "Never before, in any school, ever, had the students devoted 50% of the time to studying!" Fidel Castro continued emphasizing the need "to keep developing this approach to introduce students to production, so that our educational system will be able one day to be self-financed practically by the students' work".

The moral and physical damages suffered by this huge number of adolescents was of such magnitude that Pope John Paul II felt obliged to make a public condemnation of this educational system during his homily in the city of Santa Clara when he visited Cuba in 1998. He denounced the separation of children from their parents during their secondary and high school years. For him, the boarding-school environment was prompt to make students lose their traditional family values, resulting in the spread of promiscuous behavior, loss of ethical values, premarital sexual relations at an early age and easy recourse to abortion."[33]

A decade later, the government started dismantling the system. At the end of the 2008-2009 school year, the Cuban government announced the abolishment of this educational project. A famous blogger on the island wrote the following *Requiescat*:

> Fortunately, the experiment appears to have ended. Lack of productivity, contagion of infection diseases, lessening of ethical values and the low level of academic achievement have brought down this education method. After years of economic losses, since the students consumed more than what they were able to obtain form the soil, our authorities have convinced themselves that the best

32 Speech at the technological institute of soils, fertilizers and feeds for livestock "Rubén Martínez Villena," January 30, 1967 (http://www.cuba.cu/gobierno/discursos/1967/esp/f300167e.html).

33 http://www.americancatholic.org/messenger/apr1998/feature1.asp#F3

place for a young person to be is with his or her parents. They just announced the end of the scholarships without a public apology to those who served as guinea pigs of a failed experiment that took away part of our dreams and our health.[34]

As with most previous projects, most of the compounds lie abandoned, while others have become part of the prison system of the Cuban regime. Yes, the regime that, in 1959, converted several military barracks into schools is now using a large number of former schools in the countryside as prisons. Examples include the middle school "Lino Pérez Muñoz" in Juraguá, Cienfuegos province, now housing 500 prisoners transferred from the Ariza Prison in the same province,[35] and two in the northern area of Villa Clara province: "General Lacret" and "José Luis Robau".[36] Add 17 more in the Sierra de Cubitas municipality and the municipal facility of the Ministry of Education in Jimaguayú municipality.[37]

There were also unconfirmed reports about two more in the municipality Santo Domingo and in the Valle del Yabú, both in the province of Villa Clara.[38]

The "Blas Roca" Labor Contingent

This form of labor mobilization emerged as a replacement for the construction micro-brigades that operated in urban areas a few months after Castro proposed them on his speech of July 26, 1970, operating until the mid-1980s.[39] They were founded on October 1, 1987. During the commemoration of their third anniversary, the idea of establishing the first exclusively agricultural contingent came to the table. In October 1990, Fidel Castro announced the he had considered the contingents to be an excellent idea and thought about the best place for them given their discipline and organization: "Well, in plantain with micro jet and in

---

34 http://www.desdecuba.com/generaciony/?p=1640.

35 http://lafronteratransparente.wordpress.com/2012/05/27/escuelas-convertidas-en-carceles/.

36 http://lafronteratransparente.wordpress.com/2012/05/27/escuelas-convertidas-en-carceles/.

37 http://www.primaveradigital.org/primavera/cuba-prisiones/90-prisiones/5376-escuelas-convertidas-en-campamentos-de-trabajo-forzado.html.

38 http://cubavibra.blogspot.com/2012/06/convierten-escuelas-en-prisiones.html.

39 Those interested in the transition from the construction brigades to the Blas Roca Labor Contingent, can consult Bunck (1994: 172-173).

plantain with aerial micro jet… and immediately asked agricultural authorities to look for a whole lot of land"[40]

After that, there was nothing but praise for this type of labor mobilization. Castro later said[41] that, at the beginning, the plan was to organize only one Brigade for the agricultural sector, then he had realized that more were needed because around 16,580 acres were to be devoted to plantain production with micro jet. Then, he decided to place one of these well-disciplined Brigades wherever there was one of those plantations. That was how 20 Contingent Brigades were created. Castro also told the story[42] of the need to finish an important cold-storage facility that had been under construction for 10 years. He put the task in the hands of Brigade 16 and the job was completed. He also referred to his encounter with Brigade 30, a group that had cleaned plantain plots 12 times from December to May, which represented a tremendous effort.[43]

It was not until the end of 1992,[44] that Fidel Castro referred to the different labor units working in the country despite the hardships brought about by the Special Period. He mentioned the different building forces of the Ministry of Construction and the rest of the organisms, the "Blas Roca" Contingent, the Caribe Building Enterprise (Unión de Empresas Constructora Caribe, UNECA), the builders of Popular Power, the micro brigades, the builders from other ministries and organisms such as the Ministry of Sugar, and several others. Many of those builders, including several "Blas Roca" Contingents went to the agricultural sector.

The Cuban regime does not hide the fact that the Blas Roca Contingents also participate in repressive activities against the population. Most of the times,

---

40 http://www.cuba.cu/gobierno/discursos/1990/esp/f011090e.html.

41 Closing remarks at the provincial assembly of Havana's Communist Party, held at "Antonio Maceo" in Ceiba del Agua, Havana, on 3 February 1991: http://www.cuba.cu/gobierno/discursos/1991/esp/f030291e.html.

42 Inaugural ceremony of the cold-storage plant "Habana IV", Alquízar, on 1 April 1991: http://www.cuba.cu/gobierno/discursos/1991/esp/f010491e.html.

43 Ceremony to celebrate Peasant Day, Quivicán, 17 May 1991: http://www.cuba.cu/gobierno/discursos/1991/esp/f170591e.html.

44 Ceremony on Constructor Day, Havana, 5 December 1992: http://www.cuba.cu/gobierno/discursos/1992/esp/f051292e.html.

protests or demonstrations by opponents if the regime receive the impact of members of the Ministry of the Interior and of paramilitary groups such as Rapid Response Brigades, Committees for the Defense of the Revolution and the Blas Roca Contingents.

Chapter 7

GIANT IS BEAUTIFUL

Gigantism is not an article of Marxist faith.
Rene Dumont.[1]

When British economist E.F. Schumacher published *Small is Beautiful: A study of economics as if people mattered* in 1973 —arguing for small, appropriate technologies that empowered people—Fidel Castro had already spent almost 15 years doing the opposite. To him, "bigger is better" and people did not need to be empowered because he was there to make all the decisions. Furthermore, not only was bigger better, but giant was beautiful. The word "gigantomania" (or "gigantis") comes from the terms "giant" and "madness" used in Ancient Greek to refer to the execution of unusually and superfluously large projects. In general, it has been a common feature of totalitarian regimes such as the Soviet Union, Nazi Germany, Fascist Italy, Communist China and North Korea.[2] The following examples of giant projects make a case for the inclusion of Castro's Cuba on that list.

---

1 (1970: 55).
2 http://en.wikipedia.org/wiki/Gigantomania.

Havana's Green Belt

Project Overview

The food scarcity problem that developed in the mid-1960s, especially in the city of Havana, gave rise to a project whose cost no one can calculate. Gutelman[3] described it as a series of parcels with a total area of 840,000 acres around Havana, divided in 44 zones, administered by individual organisms of the capital city but under the control of a central entity.

Castro himself provided a general idea of the magnitude of the project during a speech where he summarized the accomplishments up to the end of the year 1968.[4] (See the book's website for the list of activities and equipment: www.cubanquixote.com).

Multitudes of city dwellers were mobilized to work in Havana's green belt. Even foreign visitors wanted to participate in this historic project. From its numerous components, I have chosen to emphasize two of them: the windbreaks and the Piccolino tractors.

The Windbreaks

In the Introduction, I refer to most of Castro's projects lacking an ending date and a performance evaluation. The windbreaks [*cortinas rompevientos*] project is a peculiar case in the long list of Castro's agricultural follies. It has a starting date and an ending date, but a failing grade. We know that information from Castro himself.

Field windbreaks are linear plantings of trees/shrubs designed to reduce wind speed in open fields, preventing soil erosion and protecting adjacent crops from wind damage. They were not Castro's invention, for farmers in many countries have used them for a long time, since their origin in Scotland in the mid-1400s. However, Castro hinted as if he had been the author of the discovery.

Castro borrowed the practice at the time he was involved in developing Havana's Green Belt intended to make the capital self-sufficient in fruits,

---

3 (1970: 234-235).

4 See http://www.cuba.cu/gobierno/discursos/1968/esp/f280968e.html.

vegetables, meat and many other food products. The problem was that all that investment was at the mercy of the hurricanes that pass over that region from time to time. His magnificent project needed to be protected. Although the agricultural technique was not his, those around him praised his intelligence when he decided to protect the area with some of Mother Nature's magnanimous gifts.

During a speech commemorating the sixth anniversary of the Committees for the Defense of the Revolution, on September 28, 1966, Fidel told the cheering crowd about the need to reckon with hurricanes and the necessity to develop windbreak curtains. He also recognized that windbreaks could not prevent fruits or grains from falling under winds of 200 kilometers [125 miles] per hour, but could protect the plantations.[5]

Exactly one year later, during the celebration of the CDRs,[6] he repeated his idea. Obviously, the work had not started yet as he confessed to be still looking for the best tree varieties to plant. In a sarcastic tone, he added, "We tell the comrades we have to develop some windbreaks so that in the middle of a cyclone anyone can sit behind a curtain and read the newspaper."

A few months later, Castro talked about the subject again.[7] He now added sugarcane plantations to the crops that would have windbreaks, which now included bananas, citrus and others. In addition, on April 19, 1968, at the seventh anniversary of the victory in Playa Girón, he returned to the subject.[8] Finally, at the next celebration of the anniversary of the CDR, on September 28, 1968, he reported the accomplishments in that regard, including fruit trees planted, forestry varieties and work on tracing and planting windbreaks.[9] (See the book's website: www.cubanquixote.com). He mentioned windbreaks of precious woods

---

5   http://www.cuba.cu/gobierno/discursos/1966/esp/f280966e.html

6   In the seventh anniversary in 38 September 1967: http://www.cuba.cu/gobierno/discursos/1967/esp/f280967e.html

7   In the regional concentration held in Sagua la Grande, Las villas, to commemorate the tenth anniversary of the April 9th 1958 strike. http://www.cuba.cu/gobierno/discursos/1968/esp/f090468e.html.

8   http://www.cuba.cu/gobierno/discursos/1968/esp/f190468e.html

9   http://www.cuba.cu/gobierno/discursos/1968/esp/f280968e.html

to preserve the humidity of the soil to make it more productive.[10] Then he was more specific: "Between the trees of precious woods we plant coffee and, on one of the sides of the curtains, we plant smaller plants to get a greater effect from the windbreak, we put a native lemon plant or a tamarind plant".

On November 15, 1968, at the inauguration of an elementary school in the Peru Valley, Jaruco Municipality, he related the windbreaks to the project he was praising:[11] "A dairy enterprise where there was nothing before and suddenly, the fence, the windbreaks curtains, and the facilities, everything…"

During the inauguration of a Policlinic in Güines, on January 5, 1969, he returned to the topic: "… the agricultural plans are already projects, and the architects are the ones working on the physical planning: tracing the roads, the windbreaks curtains, where to put the irrigation and drainage ditches, where everything goes".[12] He made it clear that "not a single of those trees can be planted if it is not protected with solid windbreaks… and the plantain plantations also must be protected with windbreaks. Our worry is that, while the curtains are growing, because the curtains need to be done with very strong trees…" He then returned to the numbers: "In the southern part of the province, where winds are strong, there will be at least 10 strips of land of 100 kilometers of windbreaks curtains. There it will be windbreaks in every kilometer in the sugarcane areas. Of course, in the plantain area that curtain would not be one kilometer long because it is divided in much shorter distances". He also mentioned that the benefit from the windbreaks would also extend to produce rain because in Cuba, the saturation level is achieved relatively fast and the increase in evaporation in many cases can generate rain.

In a speech of January 30, 1969,[13] Castro praised the type of agricultural organization in the area of Niña Bonita, like the modern one he expected to have

---

10 http://www.cuba.cu/gobierno/discursos/1968/esp/f300968e.html

11 http://www.cuba.cu/gobierno/discursos/1968/esp/f151168e.html.

12 http://www.cuba.cu/gobierno/discursos/1969/esp/f050169e.html.

13 In the inaugural act of 72 houses, an elementary school and other facilities in the Genetic Experimental Plan "Niña Bonita", Cangrejeras, Marianao.

in 1980. He described the windbreaks, the roads, the pasture areas laid out in a geometrical design. In other words, everything followed plans.[14]

During his speech of May 13, 1969, at the I Congress of Animal Science, he advised to be alert against adverse factors such as hurricanes, flooding, droughts, weeds... He believed that the latter events were solvable and that adequate windbreaks can protect fruit trees likely to suffer damage from hurricanes.[15]

Castro did not mention the windbreaks in any of his public speeches until 1991. He had gotten tired of them. Either he did not find them to be that useful or he thought that there was something better than what he had originally proposed. On February 3, 1991, at a provincial meeting of the Communist Party in Ceiba del Agua, he ended his enchantment with the windbreaks, while tractors were waiting to demolish them. He explained the reasons for his change of mind:[16]

> We are going to turn Ceiba del Agua —as we agreed more than a year ago—into a citrus orchard, where we aim to produce 200 000 tons with twice as many plants per area, with the micro jet or drip irrigation system, demolishing the windbreaks areas. Windbreaks really have proven insect hosts that steal water and light. A higher density of trees, acting as tree walls, protects better the plants.

Castro's love affair with windbreaks had ended, and he announced it in public. Now, instead of windbreak curtains, whose defects he discovered more than 20 years after building them, doubling tree density (planting trees and shrubs closer) was the solution to protect plantations from strong hurricane winds.

The requiescat appeared in early 1991. The next generation of Cubans was already coming of age and people tend to ignore Castro's speeches because they are numerous and they are full of contradictions. Therefore, after numerous speeches and written *Reflexiones*,[17] a local leader unknowingly tried to resurrect the abandoned project.

---

14 http://www.cuba.cu/gobierno/discursos/1969/esp/f300169e.html.

15 http://www.cuba.cu/gobierno/discursos/1969/esp/f130569e.html.

16 http://www.cuba.cu/gobierno/discursos/1991/esp/f030291e.html

17 See http://www.cuba.cu/gobierno/discursos/.

On June 6, 2009, on World Environment Day, a Cuban expert[18] in Havana made the proposal in a paper presented at the Institute of Forestry Research. He recalled the benefits of windbreaks mentioned by Castro and called for a return to the environmental practice. Contrary to what had prompted Castro to do away with the project, this scientist argued that windbreaks constituted living walls that diminished the incidence of plagues, contributing to the ecological balance of nearby agricultural crops. Other benefits included an increase in the supply of wood, fruits, insecticides, forage and other products that could become valuable substitutes for imports.

Three years later, members of the National Association of Small Farmers (ANAP) decided to build windbreak curtains to lessen the effects of climate changes in the Minas municipality, Camagüey province.[19] Again, they repeated their following of Castro's idea for precisely the reason he argued to eliminate them: combat insect and diseases to achieve ecological balance. More than 20 productive units were implementing this project following the original idea of the Commander in Chief two decades earlier -a costly idea he had long ago discarded, but the new generation did not know or did not want to remember!

The Piccolino Tractors

The story of these small tractors dates back to 1950, when the first two-wheeled tractor appeared on the market.[20] Five years later, the Italian enterprise Goldoni obtained exclusive commercial rights for their distribution. In 1969, the company signed an agreement covering the sale of 1,500 tractors (GM4 and "Export") to Cuba.[21] The negotiations had started prior to that date, as expressed by Castro in one of his speeches.

---

18 Arsenio Renda Sayous, The news was advanced by AIN and reproduced by Radio Angulo at http://www.radioangulo.cu/noticias/cuba/5137-abogan%20por%20retomar%20uso%20de%20cortinas%20rompevientos%20en%20Cuba.html.

19 http://vozbayatabominas.wordpress.com/2012/06/20/ejecutan-campesinos-en-minas-creacion-de-cortinas-rompevientos-para-mitigar-efectos-del-cambio-climatico/

20 More information can be obtained at http://www.b2match.eu/eima2012/participants/21.

21 http://it.wikipedia.org/wiki/Goldoni_%28azienda%29.

Castro said that, for some time, they had been eager to receive the machinery so badly needed at that time in Havana's Green Belt. Also noted that, in the period since they were acquired until their arrival in the country, the operators for the tractors had been prepared. At the graduating ceremony, Fidel stated that the arrival of the machinery had taken a little more than expected, but perhaps this has helped to give even more strength and more experience this first battalion. "And as the first battalion, of course is very important that you are well prepared".[22]

It was not farfetched to assume that "the first battalion would be followed by a second battalion" because he considered that the Belt would need between 200 and 250 tractors in need of maintenance. The process would later continue with the formation of other battalions for other crops in other parts of Havana province, among them banana and citrus crops.

He had a gigantic plan in mind for the midget tractors. After work in Havana was completed, he planned to send them to pineapple production areas, which would require five more battalions. And also to the province of Pinar del Rio, the Isle of Pines, Matanzas, Las Villas, Camagüey and Oriente; that is, for the entire country. The Milkmaid syndrome was multiplying midget tractors. Here is an excerpt of his reasoning: He said they were studying the distances. That is to see if the machines can work along the groove, and other distances to intercrop pigeon peas. However, it is important to check if this cultivation can solve problems of extensive plantation management. He was willing to sacrifice some of his goals, as is the immediate aim of obtaining a crop of a legume, precisely in order to achieve it through mechanization.

Castro added a discussion on the possibility of planting pairs of trees on lots measuring 2 by 1.70 meters, with 30 inches apart. He was planning to use that distance in the citrus groves of the following year and depend on 1300 Piccolinos to do the work.

The Piccolinos soon disappeared from the Havana's Green Belt and the rest of the country. Other more urgent endeavors needed Castro's attention —the constant in all Fidel's plans.

---

22 In the closing ceremony of the first course of Piccolino operators held in Cangrejeras on 30 September 1968: http://www.cuba.cu/gobierno/discursos/1968/esp/f300968e.html.

Evaluation

As in the great majority of his agricultural follies, after wasting huge amounts of resources, the gardens, the coffee plants, the fruit trees, the windbreakers and the rest of this gigantic experiment disappeared little by little. It was Dumont[23] who spoke of the failures of this gigantic adventure. Instead of the green belt of fruits, vegetables, tubers, bananas and fresh milk that he had proposed in his first report to Fidel Castro in June 1960, he found in 1969 all the land surrounding Havana planted with gardens, and fruit trees inter-cropped with Caturra coffee. The farmers that supplied the city became urban-rationed citizens and ceased being food suppliers.

That project lacked previous studies that could have unveiled that the humid, thin, and rocky soil was not suitable. Although the lemon trees grew strong, there were too many in the areas planted with coffee. When Dumont arrived in June 1969, the coffee plants appeared to be green because of the abundant rain but soon he saw them turning yellow.

Two other mistakes were the use of the Arabica coffee variety, for which the climatic conditions in Cuba are not optimal,[24] and the recruitment of 50,000 inexperienced workers. The requiescat phrase was born: "the coffee belt that strangles Havana, "rotten city.""[25]

The Water Works Project

Dams and More Dams

The establishment of the National Institute of Hydraulic Resources (INRH) in 1962 reflects Castro's objective that "not a single drop of water be lost, that not a drop of water reach the sea… that not a single stream or river be undammed".[26]

---

23   (1971: 100-102)

24   In his speech of September 28, 1968, Castro referred to those who considered the coffee plan a big mistake as the "skeptics –those who never believe anything– … who saw these plans as impossible ones or the product of fantasies". He added that "the worms were predicting that the coffee would not grow here, but what they can predict is that they will not drink that coffee" (http://www. cuba.cu/gobierno/discursos/1968/esp/f280968e.html). Obviously, no one did.

25   Dumont (1971: 100).

26   "El Paisaje" (1982: 52).

Cuba's Statistical Yearbook for 2011 lists 239 dams with a capacity of over 8.77 billion cubic meters,[27]–an excessive number for a small and narrow country as Cuba.

Castro's obsession with gigantomania in water works was clearly set out during his speech on October 30, 1967, when he stated that, in five years, this project would be able to irrigate 8,290,000 acres of land, which would be twice the area served by the Aswan Dam.[28] (See chapter 1).

The Río Cauto is Cuba's longest river. On May 30, 1968, Fidel Castro spoke at the inauguration of several hydraulic projects in the Cauto basin.[29] He detailed the features of this gigantic project: 281 kilometers of main, primary and secondary channels; over 6.8 cubic meters of soil to be removed from dams; channels, tunnels, wells, built within 1,199 metric tons of reinforced steel, 25,000 cubic meters of concrete, 250,000 bags of cement. More than 1,600 people worked during six months using a huge number and variety of heavy machinery and equipment.

Those were only a minor part of the figures mentioned by Castro in his speech about one of the aspects of a project that intended to bring the waters of the Cauto River to the neighboring province of Camagüey and others beyond.

Field Irrigation and Drainage

The Irrigation and Drainage Research Institute (*Instituto de Investigaciones de Riego y Drenaje -IIRD*) and the Agricultural Mechanization Research Institute (*Instituto de Investigaciones de Mecanización Agropecuaria – IIMA)* were combined in 2010 to establish the Agricultural Engineering Research Institute (*Instituto de Investigaciones de Ingeniería Agrícola – IIIA).*[30]

During his speech at the 25th anniversary of "Los Naranjos" enterprise, on May 26, 1989,[31] Fidel Castro announced that experimental results on sugarcane irrigation and field drainage (*drenaje parcelario*) had been successful.

---

27 http://www.one.cu/aec2011/esp/12_tabla_cuadro.htm. (Table 12.6).

28 http://www.cuba.cu/gobierno/discursos/1967/esp/f301067e.html.

29 http://www.cuba.cu/gobierno/discursos/1968/esp/f300568e.html.

30 http://www.ecured.cu/index.php/Instituto_de_Investigaciones_de_Ingenier%C3%ADa_Agr%C3%ADcola.

31 http://www.cuba.cu/gobierno/discursos/1989/esp/f260589e.html.

Implementation of the new techniques had been completed on almost 2 million acres and the goal was "to continue to work to expand it to other areas in a few years; it won't be 10 years, and it is possible that it will sooner than eight, it is possible it won't be more than seven…" He turned immediately to the number of Brigades being organized: "We have already 47, and 121 will be available by the end of the year, we will have 200 next year, and will try to reach 3000 in the second semester of 1991; it will be more or less around those figures." Productivity will be enhanced by the application of this technique, yielding around two extra million tons of sugar.

Although Castro had not mentioned it, this type of drainage, by controlling the water table, has the objective of avoiding or minimizing the secondary salinity induced by irrigation. It had become a problem in several countries such as Argentina, Cuba, Perú and México.[32]

On September 30, 1989, Castro announced[33] that 57 drainage Brigades were already organized. They had some trucks, harrows, bulldozers, levelers, loaders, diggers, and other machinery. The organization of 64 more was in progress and was supposed to be completed by the end of the year. He announced that there were 121 brigades working on field irrigation and drainage in the country and the goal was to have 300.

On October 10, 1991, he turned to the topic again during the inaugural session of the Fourth Congress of the Cuban Communist Party in Santiago de Cuba.[34] It was the dismal speech of the advent of the Special Period. He complained about the need to reduce the machinery and equipment needed to fulfill the goal of the field drainage project. Because of the crumbling of the U.S.S.R., imports of agricultural machinery and equipment went down to minimal loads.

This Plan was no different than others in one essential feature. After experimental results had shown positive increases in yields in 1986, five years later the

---

32 http://www.fao.org/nr/water/aquastat/regions/lac/indexesp6.stm.

33 In the third anniversary of the strenghtening of the microbrigade movement, held in Karl Marx Theater, Havana, on 30 September 1989 (http://www.cuba.cu/gobierno/discursos/1989/esp/f300989e.html).

34 http://www.cuba.cu/gobierno/discursos/1991/esp/f101091e.html.

economic analysis was still lacking. "The extensive investment involved in the application of field drainage requires that, as with any other capital-improvement measure, an economic evaluation be conducted".[35] Finally, as stated in chapter 2, Aranda[36] confirmed that Castro did not follow the advice of local technicians.

The Genetic Revolution

Since the early 1960s, Fidel Castro was obsessed with the idea of implementing a plan of genetic improvement leading to the creation of new races of livestock[37] and better feeding methods. This section contains a brief summary of some elements of that project.[38]

Early Efforts: Artificial Insemination

In 1959, Fidel Castro visited "El Dique", a center developing horses for the army that was already using artificial insemination techniques. Castro ordered to place the military unit under the National Institute of Agrarian Reform (INRA). The National Directorate of Artificial Insemination (DNIA) was born in 1960.[39] In May 1962, after paying an undetermined amount (estimates range between $28,000 and 1 million), the stallion "Rosafe Signet" (1958 Grand Royal Champion Male in Canada)[40] arrived in Cuba in the company of others. The semen extracted from this stallion was frozen and stored for future use.

---

35 Zumaquero Posada, et al. (1991: 141).

36 (1975: 42-43).

37 Although we have discussed only dairy and beef cattle –where the efforts were concentrated– Castro was also interested in developing other superior animal crosses, A short list would include rabbits, pigeons, chickens, and even buffalos.

38 The literature on this topic is very extensive, especially in terms of speeches by Castro, obsessed as he was with this idea. The information for this brief general summary was taken from his speech of January 30, 1969 during the inauguration of infrastructure at the Niña Bonita genetic experimental plan (http://www.cuba.cu/gobierno/discursos/1969/esp/f300169e.html); at the XXV anniversary of the establishment of the cattle research center at Los Naranjos in May 26, 1989 (http://www.cuba.cu/gobierno/discursos/1989/esp/f260589e.html); and at the first congress of the Institute of Animal Science on May 13, 1969 (http://www.cuba.cu/gobierno/discursos/1969/esp/ f130569e.html).

39 More information can be found in http://www.ecured.cu/index.php/Centro_de_Investigaciones_para_el_Mejoramiento_Animal_de_la_Ganader%C3%ADa_Tropical

40 http://www.holsteinjournal.com/?p=96.

Fidel Castro became a frequent visitor. He was there after learning of the serious health problems Rosafé Signet presented on April 1965. After taking the decision to put down the animal, Castro requested that the least painful method be used for that purpose. Alfonso[41] comments that the animal died from excessive ejaculations, becoming a martyr of the genetic revolution, which Montaner[42] corroborates with a death certificate that specifies the cause of death as a brain hemorrhage resulting from the millionth ejaculation. At his burial, Castro even threw a handful of soil on his grave.[43] (The press did not report if the *Comandante* had shed a tear during the solemn ceremony.) Once again, the head of the Cuban State lacked a proper sense of priorities, repeated years later when a small town in the province of Mayabeque received the name of the beloved animal.

On December 12, 1961 in a graduation ceremony, where 200 young men received their diplomas of artificial inseminators, Castro explained the rationale behind the practice:[44]

> We can grab the little cow that gives the least amount of milk in Cuba, a cow that gives half-liter, a "dry cow". If we inseminate her with a 28,000-dollar bull, the daughter will give much more milk. If we inseminate the bull's daughter or granddaughter with a bull of

---

41   (2013: 78).

42   (1994: 183).

43   Se note 45 above.

44   http://www.cuba.cu/gobierno/discursos/1961/esp/f121261e.html.

more or less the same quality, then the granddaughter gives much more milk. If we inseminate that granddaughter also with the semen of another bull of roughly similar quality, the great granddaughter will give more milk.

What should we do in 7 or 8 years? Well, that not all great granddaughters and great great granddaughters of the current cows be cows that produce two or three liters, but 15 and 20, and we can do it.

This impressive quote deserves at least a quick recalling of the fable about the Milkmaid and the Pail. However, we are going to do even better this time. It was not until recently that we learned new things about the artificial insemination program. An article published on December 14, 2011,[45] discusses the 50th anniversary of the first group of graduates in the artificial insemination technique.. The hero of the story, a peasant from Camagüey province named Evaristo Tejeda, was one of the students who enrolled in the first course at the age of 16. Today, he is a veterinary doctor. The course lasted 10 months, from February to December 1961. I became curious about the rationale for the length of the study. How would it compare with the same training in other countries? A United States publication[46] affirms that this technique can be learned in about three days' practice under professional instruction and supervision. Additional proficiency and confidence come with further work on your own. One wonders why the huge difference between three days and 10 months! Of the 1,200 who started the course, only 200 graduated. Tejeda is the only one who remains in the livestock field.

I assume that some people consider it a shame to receive the sarcastic appellative "*mamporrero*",[47] even if one uses a pistol with the semen rather than the

---

45 See "Un cortador de caña camagüeyano devenido científico," by Miozotis Fabelo Pinares, in Radio Cadena Agramonte: http://www.cadenagramonte.cu/index.php/articulos/ver/18780.

46 "Select Reproductive Solutions: A.I. technique in cattle", by Mel Delarnette and Ray Nebel (http://www.selectsires.com/resources/fertilitydocs/ai_technique_cattle.pdf).

47 According to the Spanish Royal Academy (RAE), "mamporrero" is the name given to the technician that helps the male animal in the act of copulation by directing his penis in the right direction. The Army in Cuba had a corporal *mamporrero* in every barrack with horses.

manual assistance to the animal's genital organ. The other reason for the stampede from the field could have been the result of fear generated from furious cows after realizing that they received a lousy substitute. Perhaps the Cuban press has hidden sporadic incidents like those that the "battle of the cow's stable" mentioned a few times in Orwell's *Animal Farm*.[48]

Program Overview

The first attempt at getting the genetic project off the ground took place in 1964 with the establishment of a genetic enterprise in Los Naranjos, in the area of Ceiba del Agua, Havana province. It started with 400 acres of land. Twenty-five years later, it had 100,000 acres 174 cow-houses. One of its main projects was the development of the red Holstein and the Tropical Holstein (a cow that could produce more milk, fat and protein under Cuba's climatic conditions of extreme heat), in addition to the introduction of new races, such as Aberdeen, Simmental, and others. Castro was so interested in this project that he added one more unit to his long list of residences. It is a beautiful mansion located in Los Naranjos, in Ceiba del Agua area near Caimito. A two-story rural dwelling with swimming pool and walls of bullet-proof crystals.[49]

After working with the Holstein, work expanded to include the Criollo, Brown Swiss and other races, the F-1 and F-2, the 5/8 with different combinations based on Cebú and Holstein, or other race with Holstein. Then the emphasis was on beef cattle; new crosses and combinations included races like Limousin, Criollo, Charolais, Holstein, Aberdeen, and Santa Gertrudis.

Parallel to Los Naranjos' there was another experimental genetic plan established at Niña Bonita dairy enterprise, located in Cangrejera, Marianao, Havana province. It consisted of 10 units operating in 2,000 acres. It started working with the Zebu —Cuba's main cattle race, adapted to tropical climate— in order to produce hybrids with dairy cattle.

The founding of the Institute of Animal Science complemented the plans and added value through research on topics related to animal nutrition and

---

48 Orwell (1994: 124).

49 http://www.desdecuba.com/mason/?p=6379.

livestock development. It was a peculiar center. Scientists and technicians discussed working procedures with the government and, as a result, received a certain degree of latitude to conduct their business with some freedom from the central government. Castro later stated, "Nonetheless efforts would be made to try to reconcile the directives, the ideas, and the viewpoints of the researchers with the immediate interests of the country in order to solve its most urgent needs". Given Castro's personality, an arrangement granting some autonomy to researchers could not last long.

How to feed the cattle was another issue to solve. Different countries use different means depending of climatic and other conditions.

Intensive Grazing

Intensive grazing is the application of better management practices to pasture, mainly through the rotation of cattle through numerous small paddocks, each with a water source, instead of allowing the cattle to continuously graze in one or two large paddocks.

The benefits of this practice include: more complete use of plant material, better consumption of less preferred forage plants and weeds, less hoof damage than in confinement housing, less eye irritation than in weedy pastures, more even spreading of animal waste over pastures, less nutrient run-off into streams and rivers, and more forage feed produced per acre.[50]

Intensive grazing came to Cuba in 1963, one year before the visit of French scientist André Voisin, who was preceded by the impact of his 1957 book *Grass productivity*. He and his wife arrived in Cuba in early December 1964, invited to teach a course and serve as Castro's consultant. They were treated like a royal couple. He suffered a heart attack and died in Havana on December 21, hardly three weeks after his arrival. He was buried in the vault of the Cuban Academy of Sciences.

Between 1964 and early 1967, more than 2,600 intensive grazing centers started operations. New capacities for more than 650,000 cows with their calves were established.[51]

---

50 Wilson et al. (1993: 2-3).

51 Aranda (1975: 107).

Dry Lot

A dry lot is an enclosure of limited size, usually bare of vegetation and used for fattening livestock. The Cuban government began using them around the mid-1960s, building 16 units in two to three years, with a total capacity of 55,600 animals. Aranda estimated that, making up to four rotations, it was feasible to fatten around 400,000 animals per year.[52]

The practice fell in disgrace after the 1960s. Since the year 2000, and with more emphasis after 2011, the official press has begun to write about new programs and the strengthening of existing ones.

Ubre Blanca (White Udder)

I am sure that most of the readers have not heard of this almost-magical cow. A group of foreign visitors had the following praise for Castro's pet: For weeks in 1981-82, she was daily front-page copy, a subject for songwriters, the occupant of an air-conditioned suite with special catered meals, even the recipient of a nationally televised visit from the head of state (who, according to Reuters, "seemed ecstatic as he whispered endearing words while circling and admiring her").[53]

Ubre Blanca is the name of a Cuban cow that symbolized Castro's quixotic efforts to create new races of cattle.[54] Her exact date of birth remains unknown. The cow produced 241 pounds of milk (109.35 liters) in three milking sessions on January 16, 1982 —more than four times the output of a typical cow. One month later, she produced 55,090 pounds (24,988.9 liters) of milk in 305 milking days. The cow's achievements appear in the Guinness Book of Records.

---

52 Aranda (1975: 97).

53 Benjamin et al. (1986: 151).

54 Some of the information in this section was taken from "Ubre Blanca" at http://en.wikipedia.org/wiki/Ubre_Blanca; and "Cuba: la clonación de Ubre Blanca" by the BBC Mundo (http://news.bbc.co.uk/hi/spanish/science/newsid_2007000/2007303.stm).

Ubre Blanca's prowess was Castro's topic in endless speeches as a proof of the superiority of breeding skills in a socialist society. The cow became his favorite trophy. Newspapers followed her performance very closely. Castro took visitors to her barn. It was obvious that the mind of the commander in chief was pushing the project one-step further. His was also the idea of scientists performing surgery to harvest the cow's eggs, hoping to fertilize them and implant them in other cows to create herds of milk-producing champions.

One day, without asking permission to her commander in chief, *Ubre Blanca* died. The sad event occurred in 1985, at the age of 13. The daily *Granma* published a full Obituary and Eulogy. Taxidermists stuffed the cow and put the body in a climate-controlled glass case at the entrance to the National Cattle Health Center, 10 miles outside Havana, where it remains. Her hometown of Nueva Gerona, in the Isle of Youth, honored her by erecting a marble statute in her memory.

There are songs and poems whose mockery transpired the feelings of the people about the story of *Ubre Blanca* as an allegory of Castro's rise to power, about the endless efforts and the waste of resources brought about by the dream of a genetic revolution that ended in a monumental failure. It is not farfetched to imagine Fidel thinking about the opportunity lost by the age difference between Rosafé Signet and Ubre Blanca. They lived 20 years apart. I am almost sure he dreamt about their wedding. It would have been a humble ceremony attended by all members of the press. The union of his two champions would have saved his genetic revolution.

The story did not end with *Ubre Blanca's* death. Scientists took tissue samples and froze them for cloning purposes. The order, again, came from Castro himself but, ten years later, things were not progressing as he had foreseen. In his speech to the V Congress of the Cuban Communist Party, when referring to recent advancements of science, he mentioned: "We have, for example, the cloning of animals, the future possibility that one cow that produces plenty of milk –Ubre Blanca– could be reproduced as many times as needed".[55] Cuba's efforts started in 1987, well ahead of the efforts in most countries, and Castro announced that Cuba would soon have a "prodigious descendent" of *Ubre Blanca* who would produce 100 liters of milk per day". The project was one of Castro's priorities and was conducted at the Center for Research of Animal Improvement.

Although ignored by the Cuban press, and probably the cause of one of Castro's tantrums, another cow surpassed *Ubre Blanca's* record in 1998. LA-Foster Blackstar Lucy in Cleveland, North Carolina, had a total annual output of 75,275 pounds.[56] That represents 1.366 more production than Castro's cow.

The dream of herds descendent of *Ubre Blanca* is still to become a reality. Hope, however, returned to the genetic revolution with the arrival of a shorter version.

The Midget Cows

With *Ubre Blanca* dead, the Commander in chief came up with a new idea to solve the milk-scarcity problem: produce thousands of midget cows![57] According to Boris Luis García, a Cuban molecular biologist who spoke with *The Wall Street Journal*, Castro envisioned cows with size of dogs living near homes and fed in mini-parcels with pasture grown in drawers under fluorescent light.[58]

Although official geneticists have yet to produce the first midget cow, several international news agencies announced at the end of July 2004, that Cuban

---

55 http://www.cuba.cu/gobierno/discursos/1997/esp/f101097e.htm.

56 http://en.wikipedia.org/wiki/Ubre_Blanca.

57 For a witty commentary about this issue, read the article by Carlos Alberto Montaner appearing in http://www.nuevaprensalibre.com/edicion13/reflexiones.htm.

58 Reyes (2002).

rancher Raúl Hernández, after five years of crossings, had obtained a cow 70-cm high able to produce between six and seven liters of milk per day.[59]

It occurred to Carlos Alberto Montaner that the bovine size would allow milking her with one hand while clapping with the other, "an always healthy maneuver in this type of regime". Once the udders dried out, the owners would be able to enjoy the delicious beef of the small animal, without forgetting the skin to manufacture "two pairs of shoes and a bongo to cheer up the Sunday parties".[60]

Evaluation

In summarizing the results of Castro's thirty years of genetic work, Rieff recalled that the decision to undertake a massive program of cross-breeding Holstein and Brahma cattle was taken in the late 1960s. The program goal was to obtain a cow that could stand up to tropical heat but still produce milk as copiously as northern European breeds. Castro had promised "We will produce more milk than Holland". The result was disastrous.[61] Cuba's livestock herd decreased by 30 percent in the period 1967-1987 and Castro had to recognize that the entire sector needed a "colossal shake-up" to improve its efficiency.[62] When Castro

---

59 The information appeared in many newspapers. We used the article "Logran raza de vaca enana en Cuba" by the AFP, July 27, 2004 (http://www.univision.com/content/content. jhtml?cid=429994).

60 "Fidel Castro y la vaca enana", *El Nuevo Herald*, 8 de agosto de 2004.

61 Rief (1996: 69)

62 Roca (1994: 99).

took power in 1959, there was one head of cattle for every of the over 6 million inhabitants. By 2011, it had decreased to 0.36 per capita.[63]

An appropriate parameter to measure the results of this ambitious plan to produce milk and beef is the rationing system. Rationing of most food items –including milk and beef– became official in March 1962. The initial issue of the ration booklet showed the persons who could purchase one liter of fresh milk per day: children seven years of age and under, the elderly, ill persons and pregnant women.

The original beef quota consisted of 12 ounces per person weekly for Havana residents, 8 ounces for other urban areas and 4 ounces for residents of the countryside.[64] The fresh milk quota has remained without major changes during the five decades that rationing has been in place. After almost 50 years of rationing, Havana residents receive –when available– 4 ounces of beef every 9 days, or a decrease from 48 ounces in 1962 to 13 ounces per month today.

No more information about these super cows sponsored by Castro is available. A press report, however, appears related to the genetic project and may signal a requiescat. Starting in 2003, Cuba's Alimport (food importing agency) engaged in commercial transactions with Florida cattlemen to purchase several loads of cattle intended to improve Cuba's cattle herds.

Several shipments have taken place. These purchases may signal the end of Cuba's genetic revolution. It seems the end of the tropical cows, midget cows, miraculous milk producers, the breeding of the F1 and F2 that could not advance to the next stage. American breeds have come to the rescue of the almost non-existent Cuban livestock population.

---

63 Figures computed from the statistical yearbook (www.one.cu): 4 million heads for a population of 11.24 million.

64 Álvarez (2004a: 135, 136, 141-142).

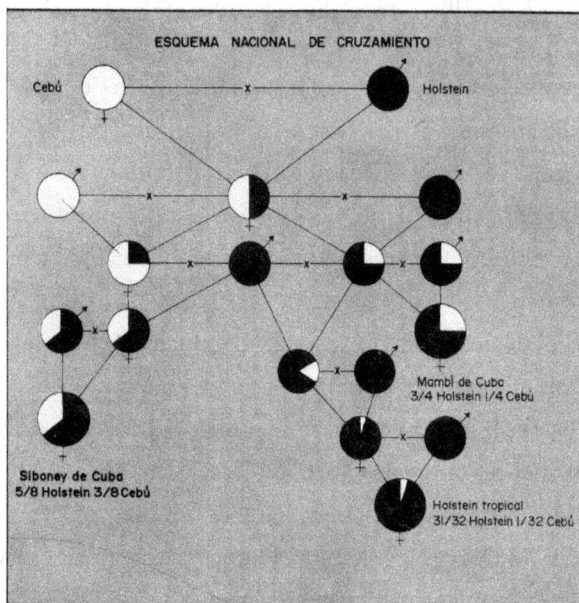

ESQUEMA NACIONAL DE CRUZAMIENTO

Cebú — Holstein

Mambí de Cuba
3/4 Holstein 1/4 Cebú

Siboney de Cuba
5/8 Holstein 3/8 Cebú

Holstein tropical
31/32 Holstein 1/32 Cebú

Epilogue

While conducting a last-minute search about a few of the topics of this book, I came across with recent startling revelations about the behavior of cows and chickens that would have helped Castro's efforts in his genetic revolution.

Let us start with the cows.[65] Research by animal behaviorists has shown that cows interact in socially complex ways, making both friends and enemies. Likewise, they mourn the deaths and even separation from those they love to the extreme of shedding tears. Their advanced cognitive abilities allow them to understand cause-and-effect relationships, enjoying intellectual challenges and getting excited when they find a solution. Each cow can recognize more than 100 members of the heard, choosing leaders for their intelligence and several other traits. Jon Watts, University of Saskatchewan researcher, states that they suffer from stress when kept on feedlots with groups greater than 200. Finally, cows value their lives and do not want to die. Perhaps for the latter reason, Castro kept beef out of the reach of his citizens.

---

65   The source is the article "The hidden lives of cows", at http://www.peta.org/issues/animals-used-for-food/factory-farming/cows/hidden-lives-cows/.

Similar behavior is attributed to chickens.[66] These animals form complex social hierarchies, also known as "pecking orders", and every chicken knows his/her place. They can remember more than 100 other birds, and have more than 30 types of sounds to distinguish between land and water threats. They present different personalities and a cultural knowledge they pass down from generation to generation.

I am not going to speculate about Castro's behavior had he been in possession of that information when posing as a geneticist. By now, the reader must be able to even surpass this writer's imagination.

The "Che Guevara" Invading Brigade

As far as we know, this farm machinery unit is the largest unit ever organized in any country in the world, or at least we have not heard of any unit of this magnitude anywhere.

Fidel Castro.[67]

It was October 30, 1967 when Fidel Castro announced proudly: "We can proclaim with joy another glorious day in the history of our fatherland: the date when the "Che Guevara" Invading Brigade started its march! Go ahead, comrades![68]

The speech reveals that, as usual, Castro was the one who had the idea and organized the project —a project so gigantic that he proudly announced it as the largest of its kind in the world. Some of the figures mentioned in his speech give an idea of the cost and destructive power of a Brigade whose main objective was to bulldoze thousands of hectares —mostly on *marabú*[69]— and to prepare the land for agricultural purposes.

---

66   "The hidden lives of chickens" can be found at http://www.peta.org/issues/animals-used-for-food/factory-farming/chickens/hidden-lives-chickens/

67   Fidel Castro, 30 October 1967, http://www.cuba.cu/gobierno/discursos/1967/esp/f301067e.html

68   Those were the farewell words of Castro's speech in the ceremony held in the area La Concepción, near the city of Bayamo, Oriente province, to initiate the activities of the Invading Machinery Brigade (http://www.cuba.cu/gobierno/discursos/1967/esp/f301067e.html).

69   See definition above.

The Brigade had 4,212 people (36 squads of 117 men each). Each squad was in charge of 20 heavy tractors and bulldozers, for a total of 720 units. No doubt about being the number one group of nature mass destruction. Still Castro was bragging about that first place!

The justification for such undertaking rests on gigantomania itself. Castro stated that "the organization of this gigantic brigade... is the result of a new concept about the manner in which to use machinery; is the result of the magnitude of the plans that we intend to carry on; is the result of the need for the clearing of lands that we still have in our country today".

Two months later, Castro spoke to the members of the brigade in the town of Jobabo, to celebrate the ending of their tasks in Oriente province, ready to start with the province of Camagüey. This time he had the numbers he lacked in his previous meeting with the brigade (See the book's website at www.cubanquixote.com).

Castro also set the schedule for that year and the following year. It is hard to image a head of State filling in a Table with the number and location of each piece of machinery and equipment and the rotation that should be executed during several months, predicting the exact month they needed to be sent to another location (See the book's website).

The result was an ecological destruction of catastrophic proportions, partially described in the Appendix.

The Ten-Million-Ton Sugar Harvest

[The imperialists] believe it is impossible, and they are convinced that a 10-million-ton harvest is impossible in a country that lacks regular sugarcane cutters... [The harvest] will be a great moral victory, a great ideological victory over imperialism, over the capitalists, over the reactionaries!

Fidel Castro.[70]

This is perhaps the most gigantic and costly project that the Cuban leader ever undertook. Castro himself announced plans for the 1969-1970 sugar campaign

---

70 Castro (1969).

several years in advance. Thomas[71] explains that "... the goal... was proclaimed for such a long time and such stress had been laid on this goal in propaganda... that it almost seemed as if the regime would stand or fall by the extent to which this target was fulfilled" The propaganda included slogans such as "What are you doing toward the ten million?", and "The ten millions will be reached." The slogans proliferated throughout Cuba on every available space.

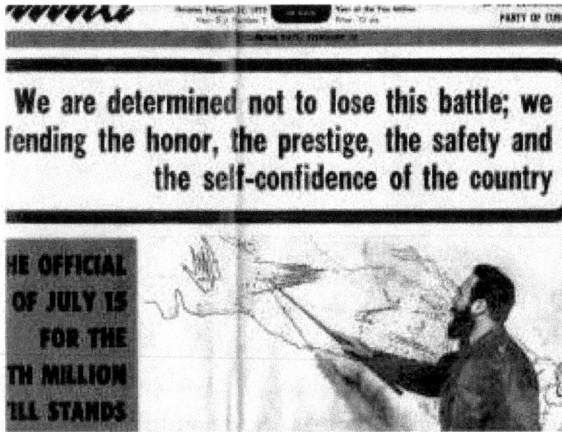

The goal was part of the Prospective Plan for the Sugar Industry, developed in the early 1960s that called for sugar production increases during the 1965-1970 period. After achieving 10 million tons in 1970, the Cuban government expected sugar production to remain at that level until 1975, and then to increase to 12 million tons. It was not until recently that some Cuban academics revealed Castro's personal role in setting the goal in a capricious and authoritarian manner, and how some economists and sugar specialists indicated almost zero possibility of achieving those goals. Castro never paid attention to the warnings. He had always believed in Dostoevsky's thinking that "the formula "two plus two equals five" is not without its attractions".[72] This time, he would make it ten. On this occasion, the pathological liar had transformed into a speedy mathematician.

---

71 (1971: 1437).

72 http://en.wikiquote.org/wiki/Fyodor_Dostoevsky.

Cuba's 2011 statistical yearbook reports an average raw sugar production of 1.25 million metric tons in the five sugar campaigns from 2002-2006 to 2009-2010, for a cumulative production level of 6.264 million metric tons.[73] Forty years after Castro's prediction, 22 harvests combined could arrive at the 28 million tons he predicted for 1980. It is interesting to note that, in a study about agricultural productivity non-state farmers were more productive than state farms (See chapter 4).[74]

The 1969 harvest became, according to Castro, "the country's agony" and totaled only 4.5 million tons.[75] Despite that signal, in his speech at the opening of the main stage of the harvest on October 27, 1969, Castro stated, "Every worker should act as he would in the face of an enemy attack, should feel like a soldier in a trench with a rifle in his hand".[76] Pérez-López[77] states, "The Prospective Plan turned out to be a monumental failure. Not only did the sugar sector failed to meet its quantitative targets in every year after 1965 —especially the much publicized 10 million ton target set for 1970— but the non-sugar economy was also adversely affected by the single-minded pursuit of expansion of sugar output."

Castro went on national radio and television in May 1970 to announce the failure of the 1970 harvest:[78] According to him, the people had not lost but won the battle. However, he recognized that the leadership had lost the battle.

He also said at that time that 9 million would be the maximum possible output since harvesting and milling activities were still taking place. Total output reached 8.5 million tons. Several scholars and specialists, however, have questioned the latter figure. For example, Thomas[79] expressed the belief that the figure "represents less than a real achievement that it will seem at first sight" for several reasons: 1. Much of the sugar came from sugarcane left over from 1969 or prematurely cut from the 1971 harvest. 2. The final figure could have

---

73 http://www.one.cu/aec2011/esp/11_tabla_cuadro.htm
74 Álvarez and Puerta (1994).
75 Thomas (1971: 1437).
76 Granma, weekly edition, November 2, 1969.
77 (1991: 13).
78 Castro (1970).
79 (1971: 1437)

been falsified and, providing that the Soviet Union assists in the deception (by, for instance, announcing that she has bought from Cuba 7 million tons), there is no means of checking the truth of the announcement. 3. Even achieving the 10 million tons goal, Cuba would still have been producing less sugar per head of population than she was in 1925. 4. The long-term costs of this grand Potemkin-type harvest are impossible to estimate.

In addition to the short- and long-term monetary costs and waste of resources, the enthusiasm of Cubans transformed into apathy due to the failure to meet the highly publicized target. A wave of disappointment swept the island. To make them believe in the power of the revolution to make things happen, Castro purged technicians and bureaucrats whom he had blamed for the failure. Once again, the responsibility for his follies fell on others.

Why would Fidel launch an unfeasible project with such degree of fanfare? Why make that effort a symbol of national pride? Finally, as in the case of many other projects, why announce the defeat or, if unavoidable, why not falsify the results?[80] Some people have a very plausible answer: Castro wanted to get rid of the minimal residues of Maoism still alive in his revolution.[81] The reason was the need to embrace the Soviet theory of 5-year economic planning. Five years after the harvest failure, it became a reality.

The Document entitled "Theses and Resolutions of the I Congress of the Cuban Communist Party – About the Party's Programmatic Platform"[82] contains countless references about Cuba's return to Soviet paternalism. It denounced "anti-communism and anti-Sovietism", stating their intention to "unveil the insidious anti-Soviet campaigns, emphasizing the decisive role of the USSR in the world struggle". It also expresses the Party's intention "to develop and

---

80 People informed about the workings of the sweeteners international market would argue that it is very difficult to fool the International Sugar Organization and the commodity specialists about the results of a season. However, Cuba would have had several means to hide the million plus that was not produced.

81 This thought appeared in the blog *Estancia Cubana* under an articles entitled "La zafra de los 10 millones e Ichikawa" by Camilo López Darias, dated March 8, 2007 (http://blogs.periodista-digital.com/estanciacubana.php/2007/09/03/la-zafra-de-los-10-millones-e-ichikawa).

82 http://congresopcc.cip.cu/wp-content/uploads/2011/03/I-Congreso-PCC.-Tesis-y-Resoluciones-sobre-la-Plataforma-Program%C3%A1tica-del-Partido.pdf.

deepen the multiple relations with the USSR", and to become a member of the CMEA. Explicit was the intention "to organize production and the rest of economic activities and to perform its planning and control". They hope "to use the accumulated experience of the Soviet Union in the building of socialism". Finally, the announcement of the first 1976-1980 5-year plan became public. Between the end of 1974 and the middle of 1976, Cuba and the USSR developed more than two dozen Protocols and Agreements that guaranteed the substantial subsidies the Cuban regime was to obtain from his return to the Soviet orbit.[83]

"Economic dependence upon the Soviet Union increased", says Manual Moreno Fraginals, a sugar scholar who lived most of his life on the island, in an interesting article.[84] Perhaps the most damaging result is the one that we will never know: "The total social and economic cost caused by the 1970 harvest may never be properly measured".

The *Pedraplenes* (Causeways)

The idea of building *pedraplenes* (causeways) was a latent on in Castro's mind. The Isle of Pines, renamed the Isle of Youth in 1978, was an agricultural priority from the beginning of the revolution. One of the early ideas was to build a 50-km highway joining the southern part of Cuba with the northern part of the small island. Dumont[85] states the "the project of a route over the sea to that isle would benefit if it were accompanied by a budget developed with seriousness concerning materials, foreign exchange and labor". The idea died in the planning process.

Castro himself referred to history of the construction of these roads since the early years of the revolution.[86] The first one was a short section connecting the mainland with the Zapata peninsula. The next joined Camagüey province

---

83 See Ginsburgs (1987).

84 "The Ten Million Ton Sugar Harvest (*La Zafra de los Diez Millones*)", by Manuel R. Moreno Fraginals and Teresita Pedraza Moreno, that can be found at http://faculty.mdc.edu/tpedraza/MMF-Ten%20Million%20Ton%20Harvest.htm.

85 (1971: 71).

86 Speech in the ceremony of establishing the Las Villas Campaign Contingent, Villa Clara, September 29, 1996 (http://www.cuba.cu/gobierno/discursos/1996/esp/f290996e.html).

with Cayo Sabinal. A major challenge was building one to Cayo Coco —a key far-ther away from the mainland. He acknowledged asking scientists about potential ecological damages. To estimate the potential cost, he brought in a few trucks, one bulldozer, one loader and one person and told him to find out how much it would cost to build one linear meter. Although Castro considered the cost rea-sonable, he told his comrades: "Do not talk about this *pedraplén* lest people think that we all are crazy; do not talk! ", giving this project a clandestine overtone. Cayo Coco lies 17 linear kilometers to the north, not visible from the mainland, and Castro ordered: "Throw in rocks and don't look forward".

When finished, it reached Cayo Guillermo on the west and Paredón Grande on the east. More *pedraplenes* followed in Las Tunas, Puerto Padre, Pinar del Río and Trinidad.

The environmental damages produced by this type of construction are hard to estimate. Part of those negative impacts are listed in the Appendix.

The State Extensive Growth Model of the 1980s

The greatest emphasis fell on the agricultural sector, especially in the sugarcane agro industry.[87] Its main characteristics included the expansion of agricultural areas; heavy cap-ital investment; high use of modern inputs, especially fertilizers, pesticides and machin-ery, and a system of incentives under the socialist principle of economic calculation.[88]

---

87 This section draws heavily on Álvarez and Peña Castellanos (2001: 9-40).

88 Economic calculation is the mixing of central planning with the necessary economic opera-tional autonomy of the productive units (*El sistema* 1981: 4).

Fidel Castro himself referred to this model early in its implementation. During a speech at the closing ceremony of the XVI Congress of the Sugar Workers Union on October 30, 1980. He stated, "We are implementing a mechanization policy, resulting in mechanizing 100% of the land preparation, more than 90% of the cultivation; we are using herbicides; fertilizer use has been multiplied more than seven times, most of the areas are irrigated with machinery and the irrigated area has been expanded".[89]

There are figures available for the sugarcane sector.[90] Land devoted to sugarcane increased from 3.95 million acres at the beginning of the 1980s to close to 4.7 millions at the end of the decade. Concerning fertilizer application, 1980 shows 758,700 metric tons (compared with 526,600 in 1975), increasing to 789,200 tons in 1989. Herbicide application changed from 2,111 tons ion 1980 (1,377 in 1975) to 2,192 in 1989. Machinery imports grew steadily during the decade, especially tractors, that experienced an increase from 68,294 in 1980 to 76,783 in 1989, despite the fact that they had experienced an increase of 32.4% during the previous decade.

Although the model showed some progress in increasing total production, it resulted in higher costs and irreversible damage to the environment.

Placing this gigantic effort at the end of this chapter is meaningful indeed. When the 1980 decade was approaching the finish line, the Cuban leadership realized that the model was "exhausted" for several reasons: First, its inability to increase production areas and input levels, and/or absorb increasing levels of costs to maintain current production levels. Second, it did not solve the problems of stimulus, efficiency, and others related to the economic management of the industry. Coupled with the disappearance of the socialist bloc and increasing pressures from the United States, gave birth to a series of timid reforms initiated in 1993. They started at the outset of the "Special Period in Time of Peace".

---

89 http://www.cuba.cu/gobierno/discursos/1980/esp/f301080e.html
90 Álvarez and Peña Castellanos (2001: 11-18).

Evaluation

Jacques Chonchol, the Chilean economist who worked in Cuba in the early years of the revolution, was a harsh critic of this approach.[91] His criticism of giganto-mania adopted in peoples' farms lists several negative characteristics. In addition to being a very expensive proposition, it is an inefficient distribution of investments, which hinders efficient management and control. It relies on insufficient administrative personnel and excess of centralization. In terms of labor, the salaried workers of the farm remained so, without an active participation in the enterprise. In addition, it involves high transportation costs, lack of control of animals, and other disadvantages. He ended his evaluation with the following statement: "The former makes us think that the myth that the peoples' farm, because it is a great state enterprise in a socialist economy, "is a superior form of production", will be seriously proved to be wrong in the concrete Cuban situation".

René Dumont had the hardest criticisms and they focused on ideology. It was wrong to establish not State farms but overlarge administrative farms. Marxism condemns *microfundia* but does not praise gigantism.[92]

For these giant projects to succeed, exceptional organizational capabilities and resources were necessary. Cuba had neither. The huge subsidies from the Soviet Union did not change the outcomes. Cuba still lacked organization. Its only organizer believed to be in possession of the monopoly of knowledge. The results more than corroborate that he was wrong.

91 Chonchol (1963:123-126).
92 (1970: 55).

Chapter 8

THE LAST GIANT: FOOD PROGRAM -
THE PROJECT OF THE SPECIAL PERIOD

... To solve the terrifying problem of having to eat every day.
Catholic University Association (1957).[1]

*I*n September 1990, anticipating the hardships on the Cuban economy as the result of the demise of socialism in the Soviet Union and Eastern Europe, the Cuban government announced the establishment of a "Special Period in Time of Peace", aimed at a better management of scarce resources and measures to survive the expected crisis. Food scarcity awakened the minds of the Cuban leadership to new ideas. This section discusses a measure that signaled the death of gigantomania: the food program (or *Plan Alimentario* – *PA*). The project's design dated from the so-called process of rectification of errors and negative tendencies.

General Characteristics

That the program was Castro's invention is obvious. Roca stated, "The PA shows quite clearly the marks of the Cuban President in both its strategic design and its operational detail".[2] The PA was the result of the realization by the Cuban government that the quantity and quality of food supplies had been deteriorating since

---

1 Gastón et al. (1957: 25).
2 (1994: 99).

the closing of the free peasant markets in 1986 and the establishment of the Special Period in 1990. The Fourth Congress of the Cuban Communist Party, held in October 1991, reached a consensus on the need to mitigate food scarcity.[3] In his speech delivered at the closing ceremony, Fidel Castro expressed the importance of the PA, "We will continue our programs under any circumstances, the food program receiving top priority, despite the lack of animal feed and fertilizers".[4]

What was really the PA? What were its goals and objectives? As usual (it could not be otherwise), it was a giant project. For example, a partial list of its scope includes 450,000 acres devoted to rice, a production goal of 2 million liters of milk, 68,000 tons of vegetables, tubers, and fruits to distribute to consumers in the city of Havana, and many others. As customary, costs, profitability and other efficiency indicators had no value. The needed machinery and equipment was beyond the government's means: 880 ground levelers and 300 bulldozers for the recently created forty rice production brigades.[5]

If the physical targets and the necessary machinery and equipment were obvious bottlenecks, labor would prove to be even more difficult to obtain. According to Enríquez,[6] major mobilizations took place, dozens of labor camps were established, and even building forty new communities to house worker contingents were in the plans of the countryside. These communities would offer housing, stores, health-centers, day care, schools, swimming pools, and so on.

Despite modest increases in some vegetables and tubers –infinitesimal when compared with the resources invested– most of the targets went unfulfilled. Still full of enthusiasm in July 1994, Castro asserted, "the food program continues to be the number one priority for the country, and don't you believe that we have made limited efforts on food production".[7] The truth is that the PA was already

---

3 Partido Comunista (1991).

4 Speech delivered at the closing ceremony of the IV Congress of the Cuban Communist Party in Santiago de Cuba, October 14, 1991 (http://www.cuba.cu/gobierno/discursos/esp/1991/f141091e.html).

5 Roca (1994: 98, 99).

6 (1994: 27-28).

7 Speech of July 15, 1994 (http://www.cuba.cu/gobierno/discursos/1994/esp/f150794e.html).

agonizing. As with most of the gigantic plans, a death certificate is missing and the exact date of the tragic event remains a mystery. The only official reference is contained in the document prepared for discussion by the V Congress of the Cuban Communist Party in October 1997: "The series of transformations and the accomplishments until the Special Period would have allowed the successful development of the food program designed during the period of rectification of errors and negative tendencies." Although the document acknowledges the presence of inefficiency, paternalism and other malaises,[8] Castro's recognition of the PA failure is yet to come.

Micro jet Irrigation

There are five main systems for applying water to plantains and bananas, namely: (1) flood or furrow; (2) over canopy sprinklers; (3) under canopy sprinklers, (4) micro jet of micro spinners; and (5) drip irrigation. Most countries are now using micro-irrigation systems, including micro spinner, micro jet, and drip or trickle irrigation.[9]

Cuban television reported on September 25, 1990 that Fidel Castro had visited several cooperatives in Havana province.[10] They included citrus orchards in the area of Ceiba del Agua, with micro jet irrigation. The claim was that up to 30 tons of fruit per hectare were expected. In Artemisa, Castro visited a banana plantation, with surface micro jet irrigation, announcing that 16,580 of the 20,000 acres on bananas by the end of the year would be produced with surface and air micro jet irrigation systems with higher yields and considerable water savings.

News coverage of the new irrigation technique continued on November 6, 1990 with another Fidel Castro's tour of camps in Havana province.[11] Castro complained that plantains were not suitable for student labor because of the handling distance, its technical nature, and requirement of a permanent workforce.

---

8 Proyecto (1997).
9 Robinson and Galán Saúco (2010: 182).
10 http://lanic.utexas.edu/project/castro/db/1990/19900925.html.
11 Source Line: FL0611170090 Havana, Tele Rebelde Network in Spanish 1130 GMT, 6 Nov 90.

Castro pointed out that the problem of agriculture would be primarily one of labor force.

He also visited other Food Program sites.[12] He noted that the only risk affecting large crops would be hurricanes because of their nature and the very large size of the investment. He pointed out that studies had been conducted to determine what must be done immediately after a hurricane hits.

Although the drip irrigation method coexisted with the micro jet system in Cuba's citrus orchards, the technique was used mainly on plantains. Fidel Castro was its main promoter, something that becomes clear after reading the following evaluation he gave:[13] "A plantain with aerial micro jet has an area of 4.4 square meters; that is, with twenty plus square meters we would have five seedlings, and one seedling with aerial micro jet can produce up to 150 pounds per year. With good care, good cultivation, these lands can produce enough for self-sufficiency and surpluses, although it is not an easy task for all these factors, I explained: seeds must be optimal, adequate, resistant to pests, heat, disease and optimum care, irrigation, everything."

After that, the numbers started flowing from his mind: "We have 38 000 hectares with irrigation for these crops, this means almost 100,000 acres; now we are going to add 10,000 acres more. Every citizen of Havana and Havana Province will have 154 square meters of *viandas* and vegetables, with two crops obtained from a significant portion." Therefore, micro jet plantains and bananas had a special role to play in the Food Program.

On May 17, 1991, he was touching on this topic again,[14] pondering, "How are the plantain fields doing, plantain with superficial or aerial micro jet? They are advancing, but they do not yield plantains immediately... not until one year after planted, which requires tremendous efforts." He then referred to an encounter with members of the 30th Brigade of the Blas Roca Contingent that, between December and May, had cleaned plantain fields 12 times!

---

12 http://lanic.utexas.edu/project/castro/db/1990/19901106.html.

13 In the inauguration of the cold-storage facility in Alquízar, 1 April 1991: http://www.cuba.cu/gobierno/discursos/1991/esp/f010491e.html.

14 In the ceremony to conmemórate Peasant Day, Quivicán, 17 May 1991: http://www.cuba.cu/gobierno/discursos/1991/esp/f170591e.html.

In that same speech, he stated that they were working with the most modern technique available, but it was costly. Developing 1,700 acres of plantain with aerial micro jet is like building a city. Each lot of 33 acres needs more than 800 wooden posts and a very large number of miles of underground piping and aerial hoses.

Soon after, a major natural disaster hit Cuba. On March 13, 1993, the so-called "Storm of the Century," with wind gusts surpassing the wind speed of a hurricane, provoked enormous losses in urban and rural areas. Among the crops most affected were entire banana plantations.[15] Shortly after that, Tropical Depression 1 struck Cuba in May and June 1993.[16] Then, on June 29 and 30, 1994, tropical depression Alberto struck the western part of the island.

On August 3, 1994 when Castro discussed these natural phenomena in an address to the National Assembly of People's Power:[17] "Yes, we had natural disasters. Who cannot speak of the natural disasters! Havana's plantain crops were producing more than 300,000 quintals; they were on their way up. Production went down to almost zero as the result of phenomena out of man's control. We have lost too much time in trying to rescue those plantain farms and meet the same production level. A lot of grass has grown, and cutting it caused damage to the micro jets. We have had a whole series of subjective problems so we must wage a great battle against them. We must also wage a great battle, seeking variants, alternatives concerning objective problems."

There has been no official explanation about the failure of the micro jet project. It is a successful agricultural practice in many countries of the world.[18] As an expert stated at an international micro-irrigation congress, "The success or failure of a micro-irrigation system depends to a large extent on careful selection,

---

15 http://www.cubahurricanes.org/history-hurricanes-chronicles.php.

16 http://en.wikipedia.org/wiki/Tropical_Depression_One_%281993%29.

17 http://lanic.utexas.edu/project/castro/db/1994/19940803-1.html.

18 For example, a 1990-1993 study by the USDA's Agricultural Research Service in Puerto Rico documented the economic benefits of this type or irrigation for plantains and bananas in Puerto Rico. The interesting fact is that this production increase took place on previous sugarcane lands and has translated in huge increases in profits form a 25% increase in irrigated water (http://www.ars.usda.gov/sp2UserFiles/Place/66350000/BananaIrrigation.pdf).

thorough planning, accurate design and effective management."[19] From the experiences detailed in this book, it is not difficult to blame Castro's plan for lacking all four of them.

A famous Cuban blogger,[20] who as a student worked in one of these plantations, revealed that the plants yielded huge and bland fruits, whose skins exploded due to the disproportionate internal growth. She ended: "In our plates, the watery plantains could not satisfy our hunger; neither get the country out of the crisis."

---

19 Keynote address at the opening of the 7th International Micro-Irrigation Congress in Kuala Lumpur, Malaysis. The paper entitled "Micro-irrigation: world overview on technology and utilization" was authored by F.B. Reinders: http://www.cuba.cu/gobierno/discursos/1991/esp/f170591e.html.

20 Yoani Sánchez. See http://lageneraciony.com/cultivos-de-ciclo-corto/?cp=1.

Chapter 9

SELECTED ADDITIONAL PLANS

The policy that is being followed is an agricultural development policy, and in sufficient quantity and quality to resolve all supply problems.
Fidel Castro.[1]

The plans and projects already discussed under some type of classification do not represent an exhaustive list. This chapter describes additional ones and lists others at the end.

Cayajabos Terraces

Located in the Sierra del Rosario, to the west of Cordillera de los Órganos in Pinar del Río province, Dumont called them "monumental terraces", and we owe him the technical information about this failed plan.[2]

The plan started around 1967 or 1968 in an area east of Cayajabos. One of its objectives was "to dominate the mountain" with the development of terraces to combat erosion. Dumont calls it an "experience" rather than a "systematic experiment" because only parallel terraces with level curves were in the project. Huge bulldozers traced four-meter terraces with about 10 meters of vertical drop between them. After building 100 miles of such terraces there was no idea of

---

1 Speech at the V national plenary of the Federation of Cuban Women, Sandino Stadium, Santa Clara, Las Villas, December 9, 1966. (http://www.cuba.cu/gobierno/discursos/1966/esp/f091266e.html).
2 Dumont (1971: 136-138).

the cost involved. Dumont's suggestion of smaller and closer terraces did not prosper. Then came the rains of June 1969 to prove him right, but the resources had already been wasted.

Osmani Cienfuegos, brother of the legendary commander Camilo Cienfuegos, was in charge of the Plan Sierra del Rosario. The terraces were planted with trees of precious wood (that will not grow well isolated) with coffee plants between them. His suggestion of looking for an alternate crop was not successful because "the order of planting coffee came from above." The whole operation was feasible without the terraces but, as Dumont states, "that would be less spectacular".

In the meantime, Fidel Castro was involved in raising the profile of the Plan. In his 1969 annual speech to commemorate the events of March 13, 1957, he made a surprising announcement:[3] there were 30 students becoming specialists in the engineering of mountain terraces studying in a new university close to their place of work.

By the end of 1969, Castro was already making plans well beyond the available possibilities.[4] Castro envisioned the rice industry of the future relying on plane terraces, that he thought was the optimal land use for the most productive varieties. He even mentioned the possibility to making the water movements thorough mechanized and automated floodgates.[5]

As it happened with most of his plans, Castro changed his mind about Cayajabos. The focus of the project shifted from agriculture and forestry to tourism.[6] Cottages appeared instead of terraces and the natural beauty of the area is now attracting tourists that can contribute foreign exchange. Ex-minister Cienfuegos continued in charge of the Terrazas de Cayajabos area (it is not Plan Sierra del Rosario anymore) and the small village grew due to the impact of tourism.

---

3 http://www.cuba.cu/gobierno/discursos/1969/esp/f130369e.html.

4 In the commencement ceremony of 244 students of the Economics Institute at the University of Havana, held at the CTC Theatre, on 20 of December 1969.

5 http://www.cuba.cu/gobierno/discursos/1969/esp/f201269e.html.

6 http://www.revistasexcelencias.com/caribe/viajar-viajar-viajar%E2%80%A6/destino/las-terrazas.

The newspaper *Juventud Rebelde* published an article to celebrate its 40th anniversary, explaining its current nature but without telling the reader what happened to the original plan.[7]

The Hydroponic Project

Hydroponic cultivation consists of growing crops without soil in soluble fertilizers. In 1960, the government built, at enormous expense, a vast hydroponic enterprise in Los Pinos, San Cristóbal municipality, Pinar del Río province.

Castro made a public reference to this project during a closing ceremony held in Havana's Sports Auditorium on November 8, 1960.[8] He announced the existence of a ("practically finished") people's farm with the first hydroponic vegetable cropping system to produce year-round. He had to make another prediction: "Next year, we will have vegetables all year."

Almost thirty years later, on July 12, 1988, Castro expressed again interest in the production of hydroponic crops. His objective had not changed: to provide fresh vegetables and other popular crops the entire year to the population.[9] Castro emphasized that the current plans were not ambitious enough. According to Esteban Lazo, first secretary of the Communist Party in the province of Santiago de Cuba, there were 50 hydroponic units with an area of 125 acres of land devoted to that effort.

The unavoidable question is, as always, what happened to the huge hydroponic enterprise established in Los Pinos almost 30 years before?

Angola Pigeon Peas (Guandul)

The idea of a plan to grow Angola pigeon peas, or *guandul* was launched by Castro himself during a speech on December 12, 1961. After explaining his experiment with three different types of legumes, he challenged the audience to repeat his work on every farm and cooperative.

---

7 http://www.tvcamaguey.co.cu/index.php?option=com_content&view=article&id=23211: las-terrazas-comunidad-de-referencia-nacional-en-cuba&catid=63:cuba&Itemid=79

8 http://www.cuba.cu/gobierno/discursos/1960/esp/f081160e.html.

9 http://lanic.utexas.edu/project/castro/db/1988/19880707-2.html.

He referred to the crop again on May 18, 1967. He emphasized that he had been recommending planting the grain intercropped with coffee. "Guandul is not a crop, it is a plant that protects the soil from erosion, and produces a grain that can be consumed by humans or by hens, swine, or whatever."[10]

The enthusiasm he generated got to the point that, in a conversation with students, he asked them what they would be planting on their school's communist plot. The unanimous response was: guandul!, despite the rocky nature of the plot.[11]

Quirk[12] relates Castro's debate with foreign scientists during the I Congress of Animal Science mentioned above. Following a few experiments in a pot, Castro had announced that guandul was the solution to Cuba's food needs after the failures of Pangola grass and the alfalfa experiments. Thousands of volunteers were recruited to plant the shrubs. By 1967-1968, Angola pigeon peas had proliferated throughout the island.

The plants, however, did not produce very much. Worse than that, livestock as well as humans, rejected the peas. Any farmer would have told him that the cattle would rather starve and that humans did not like them. However, Castro would not listen.

During a conversation with Reckord,[13] Dr. Willis referred to "the recent guandul fiasco" due to Fidel Castro's ignorance. Livestock rejected the peas and those who ate it became ill. Cuban *campesinos* traditionally planted guandul hedges to keep cattle off their grounds. In this case, "Fidel needed a magic feed, so some little Lysenko[14] came up with this one. The program folded." Reckord states that many people corroborated the story Dr. Willis had told him.

In 2002, a wire from the Associated Press[15] reported that the largest shipment of dry peas from Washington State and North Dakota, after the embargo

---

10   http://www.cuba.cu/gobierno/discursos/1967/esp/f180567e.html.

11   Speech of 15 March 1968 at http://www.cuba.cu/gobierno/discursos/1968/esp/f150368e.html.

12   (1993: 627).

13   (1971: 148-149).

14   Trofin Lysenko (1898-1976) was a Soviet biologist and agronomist of Ukranian origin. He favored hybridization rather than Mendelian genetics.

15   http://www.cubanet.org/CNews/y02/jun02/18e3.htm In June 18.

was imposed in 1962, had been sent to Cuba. In addition to the 5,000 metric tons, sold for $1.1 million cash, Cuba was also importing 170,000 metric tons of peas from Canada.

Again, a question arises about the Angolan green peas Fidel Castro was growing in 1967-68; did they go back to their mother country?

Tropical Kudzu

It was in a speech during a graduation ceremony held on December 18, 1966, when Castro stated: "There are other legumes, such as the so-called tropical kudzu, referred to a lot in recent times. This legume grows in climates similar to Cuba's, thriving under the most difficult conditions and showing considerable productivity. By next year, we will have planted between 165,800 and 200,000 acres of legumes for pasture. With kudzu, unlike alfalfa, the problem of seed is now nonexistent."

The tropical kudzu did not produce the miraculous yields that were expected. However, during the closing ceremony of the III National Congress of the National Association of Small Farmers (ANAP), on 18 of May 1967, Castro was still insisting on the merits of the crop:[16] "Pangola with kudzu, that is what is missing in your land; there, you have to plant one row of kudzu and one row of pangola in order to avoid applying nitrogen, and you will have a much better feed… Evidio is producing 110 liters of milk with eight cows, with eight heifers that are giving him an average of 13 liters of milk feeding his cattle guinea with kudzu. Evidio is a farmer from San Andrés."

An economist working in Cuba at the time reported the planting of almost 50,000 acres of the crop.[17]

The testimony of Haroldo Dilla Alfonso reveals facts never included in the official press, let alone in Castro's speeches.[18] He recalls his mobilization, while still an adolescent, to an agricultural area in the province of Pinar del

16 http://www.cuba.cu/gobierno/discursos/1967/esp/f180567e.html
17 Aranda (1975: 90).
18 See the article "Del "kurfú" a la moringa" published on August 6, 2012 in http://cubafood.blogspot.com/2012/08/del-kufru-la-moringa.html.

Río as member of a "special Brigade" to perform a task ordered by Castro himself. The plan was to plant a legume to feed cattle. Hundreds of young people and an impressive amount of machinery were pulling tubers and roots already planted to replace them with kudzu. The commissary of the group explained the historical significance of the project directly under the leader maximum of the revolution, who showed up an afternoon along with numerous other officials to check the progress of his project. Some members of the Brigade were planting. Others were weeding with their hands, areas where the legume was already hidden below the weeds. The brigade members left two months later to never hear a word about the work they had performed. Months later, Dilla saw the commissary in a citrus grove in another province and asked him about the kudzu project. The report was simple: the plan had not made any progress, blaming the failure on the cattle for refusing to eat the legume. "It seems that it is very sour", was his excuse. In addition, perhaps, the student thought, the cows were not revolutionary militants.

The Rectangle and Triangle Projects

The "rectangle plan" of Camagüey (there was also a "triangle plan" for dairy cattle), intended to fatten beef cattle in a rectangular area of 432,500 acres, started with the work of dozens of bulldozers destroying *marabú*, but also existing pastures and fences with the goal of clearing the land to start from scratch.

It began on April 12, 1969 in Palo Quemado, Camagüey province, with other facilities in Guáimaro, in the same province. Throughout the years, the plans changed objectives to the point that today the names are part of political sub-divisions dealing also with livestock but the original project disappeared sometime without official announcement.

Although Fidel Castro never claimed to be a direct descendent of Euclid – the father of geometry—many sympathizers affirmed that he was immersed in the development of a "trapezoid plan" that, years later, would create, not a new man, but a new cow: the midget cow! It seems that the pair of opposite sides parallel of the geometric figure did not end up as expected due to unknown reasons.

The Torula Project

Torula is a yeast. In the case of Cuba, it is produced through the fermentation of sugar. Each ton has at least 46% protein but can achieve up to 52%. On July 29, 1977, Fidel Castro inaugurated the first of 10 plants. The ceremony took place in the sugar mill "Antonio Sánchez" in Cienfuegos province.[19] All plants were expected to be operating by the end of 1978.

The Cienfuegos factory, informed Fidel, was one of six of French technology and four came from Austria. Departing from a tradition of secrecy concerning costs, Castro said that the factory had a cost of US$ 5.34 million in foreign exchange and 4.79 millions in Cuban pesos.

Years later, Castro explained the economic rationality behind those plants.[20] The torula yeast was part of a barter agreement whereas the Democratic German Republic sent dry milk in exchange for torula yeast at the 1:1 rate. The agreement ended after the fall of the Berlin wall.

Several years later, the fate of the Torula Plan became public in an indirect manner. On December 24, 2010, the Cuban press[21] reported that the Cienfuegos plant was undergoing repairs at a cost of 11.2 million pesos and US$ 5 million. They said more. The report included the fact that this is the only factory of French technology that remains operating in the country, which means that the other five are closed. No mention was made of the four with Austrian technology. That is a good indication of the fate of the Torula Plan.

Other Projects

It would have a long and tedious task to describe the other plans that Fidel Castro's fertile imagination developed during his years as leader of Cuba's agricultural sector. Missing from the list are: national plans (the swine plan; the citrus plan; the coffee plan; the forestry plan; the poultry plan; the flower plan; the

---

19 http://www.cuba.cu/gobierno/discursos/1977/esp/f290777e.html.

20 Inaugural sesión of the IV Congress of the Cuban Communist Party in Santiago de Cuba, 10 October 1991 (http://www.cuba.cu/gobierno/discursos/1991/esp/f101091e.html).

21 http://www.tvcamaguey.co.cu/index.php?option=com_content&view=article&id=7082: avanza-reparacion-capital-de-planta-de-torula-en-cienfuegos&catid=63:cuba&Itemid=79.

zeolite plan); regional rice plans (Bayamo rice plan; Batabanó rice plan; "Antonio Maceo" Special Plan in Pinar del Río); the Juraguá project (not the nuclear plant but the one for fruits and vegetables); and many, many, many others.

A Final Word

It would be an exaggeration to say that everything that Castro proposed and executed failed, for there were a few successful projects. A good example is the artificial insemination project.[22] Moderate enthusiasm was expressed by Dumont for the Pangola prairies and the irrigation works, which he considered very promising despite some errors. Time would prove him wrong, however, as those projects joined the others in the list of costly efforts, most of them abandoned.

---

22 I was able to confirm that during an academic trip to Cuba in early November of 1987. While visiting research and production centers in La Habana province with two local friends, we stopped at the artificial insemination center located in Los Naranjos. The Center Director explained us almost everything about the research and empirical applications of the work they conducted. When we entered the air-conditioned stable, housing the seminal bulls, he commented that the people complained because they had to suffer Cuba's hot weather while the bulls were enjoying air conditioning. They later understood that those were expensive bulls, used to the cool Canadian weather, and represented a heavy investment for the Cuban economy.

Chapter 10

FROM GIANT TO DWARF:
THE SUGAR INDUSTRY

As we all know, Cuba is the first producer of cane sugar in the world. We have occupied that place during a long time, and, of course, we are not considering handing it to anybody.
Fidel Castro.[1]

Castro's statement in 1964 today resounds with an ironic tone. From the top priority industry, it descended to one at the bottom. It may sound funny – and, for some people, inappropriate— but his dismantling of the sugar industry is only feasible in Fidel Castro's surrealistic world. In fact, he has shown to have more imagination than Walt Disney in Snow White and the Seven Dwarfs, and more quantitative ability than Pythagoras, the first great mathematician. As we have seen many times, he can turn thousands into seven or the sevens into thousands.

After being among the leading world producers, the major employer and main source of foreign exchange for most of the twentieth century, Cuba's sugar industry finally became the victim of an unwise and capricious decision. No one questions the need to reduce its size to make it more productive and competitive; the problem is its implementation. This chapter[2] intends to give the reader

---

1   Speech of September 19, 1964, at http://www.cuba.cu/gobierno/discursos/1964/esp/ f190964e.html.

2   Unless otherwise specified, most of the material in this chapter was published by the author as an EDIS Document (Álvarez 2004b): http://edis.ifas.ufl.edu/fe472. My thanks to UF-IFAS for permission to reproduce parts of the report.

an idea of the magnitude of the project, the process of decision-making, and its implications for Cuba as an economic entity and a nation.

The Decision

The scenario was the University of Havana. The date was November 17, 2005. The setting was the commemoration of the 60th anniversary of Castro's admission to the University of Havana's Law School [No personality cult involved]. During his speech, after reiterating that he had the power to give orders to the members of the Cabinet, he recalled how he had made the important decision of dismantling most of the entire Cuban sugar industry, as if it were his private property: "I called the Minister [of sugar] and I told him, "Tell me please, how many hectares are ploughed?"" The answer, "Eighty thousand". My response was, "Not one hectare more". That was not really up to me, but I had no option; you just cannot let the country go down the tubes, and in April, I was looking at 663,200 acres of land that would be undergoing plowing."[3]

The Underlying Reasons

On April 10, 2002, the Cuban government announced that about half of Cuba's 156 sugar mills were to cease operations permanently as part of a restructuring process. Such a radical decision had to come from the very top of the Cuban leadership. In a 2003 speech, Cuba's Vice-President Carlos Lage [purged by Raúl Castro in 2009 along with the Ministry of Foreign Relations Felipe Pérez Roque because, according to Fidel, had been "seduced by the honey of power"], stated that, "as we advance on this task, we understand better Fidel's vision when he decided to close 70 mills and start this profound and broad transformation".[4] Reasons for such a drastic measure included depressed prices and a negative outlook for the world sugar market, and excess capacity in Cuba's sugar agro industry, well above current and future needs.

---

3   From his speech at the celebration of the 60th anniversary of Fidel Castro's admission to the University of Havana, November 17, 2005 (http://www.cuba.cu/gobierno/discursos/2005/ing/f171105i.html). The contrast between his concern for conservations contrasts sharply with his launching of the Che Guevara Invading Brigade discussed below.
4   Varela Pérez (2003).

José Álvarez, PhD.

General Overview

According to the Cuban Minister of Sugar,[5] the restructuring consisted of the following tasks: 1) From the existing 156 sugar mills, 71 will produce raw sugar; 14 will produce raw sugar and molasses intended for animal feed; and the remaining 71 will be deactivated (five converted into museums, five will remain idle, and 61 dismantled);[6] 2) Sugarcane production would occupy 1.73 million acres of the best soils, with the goal of achieving crop yields of 54 metric tons per hectare from harvests lasting only 90-100 days; 3) Molasses production would come from 314,700 acres of sugarcane; 4) Sugar production would satisfy domestic need of 700,000 tons, allow fulfillment of trade agreements, and the market when prices are favorable; 5) Extensive soil testing on land taken out of sugarcane production (3.4 million acres) will determine which areas should go into mixed crops, livestock, fruit trees, and forestry, which had begun in 1998;[7] 6) The Ministry of Sugar (MINAZ) would remain in operations, as promised by Castro himself.[8] (On November 11, 2011, it was announced officially that MINAZ would disappeared and "Grupo Azcuba" would be in charge of sugar, electricity and by-products production.)[9]

Deactivating the sugar mills displaced 213,000 workers: 123,540 (58%) remained in the Ministry's enterprises; 42,600 (20%) became full-time students; 21,300 (10%) moved into non-sugar agricultural production; 17,040 (8%) retired or went into some other type of business; and 8,520 (4%) worked full time dismantling the inactive sugar mills.[10] The surplus workers who opted for full-time study continued receiving their paychecks during the retraining process.

---

5 Rosales del Toro (2002: 4-5).
6 For a detailed break-down, see Álvarez (2004b); Pérez-López and Álvarez (2005).
7 MINAZ (1999).
8 http://www.cuba.cu/gobierno/discursos/2002/esp/f211002e.html.
9 http://www.cubadebate.cu/noticias/2011/11/11/grupo-azcuba-respondera-por-produccion-azucarera-y-derivados-en-la-isla-gaceta/
10 Peters (2003: 9).

The Cuban Minister of Sugar stated publicly that the remaining sugar mills would be open to foreign investment.[11] Although some intentions were reported right after the offer, the truth is that nothing serious materialized.

Scope and Regional Impact

The figures mentioned above, however, do not tell the whole story. First, milling capacity was in fact reduced and most inefficient mills were dismantled, and some provinces were affected more than others. The impact on employment was by no means small. Shortly after the official announcement, Cuba's President Castro himself had to address the nation to calm the worries of the nearly 100,000 workers about to lose their jobs.[12] However, the nation's fear was a logical reaction since Cuba's raw sugar mills were located in 100 of its 169 municipalities. While displaced workers receiving retraining could escape major impacts, workers engaged in indirect activities were to feel the repercussions of the process for a long time.

Analyses of the impact of the restructuring on the rural landscape and communities conducted early in the process was very revealing.[13] So important were the mills to the economic and political life of their regions that the small urban centers that developed around the sugar mills became the seat of government [*cabecera*] of their municipalities. Seven of these 29 mills disappeared as the result of restructuring. Even more important than on the *cabeceras* was the impact on the *batey*, or the hub that existed because of the presence of a sugar mill that contained commercial buildings, public and religious centers and family dwellings. While travelling in Cuba to study the sugar industry restructuring process, a foreign specialist wrote: "The mills and *bateyes* became modern over time, but many are centuries old… Asked about the building date of a mill in Artemisa …, its director responded, "Around 1700". His reference to the original settlement rather than the mill now standing reveals the deep ties between the industry, its

---

11 Frank (2002a).

12 Frank (2002b).

13 Álvarez and Pérez-López (2006).

people, and Cuba's distant past. The *bateyes*… are the places that are withstanding the worst of the sugar industry's restructuring."[14]

In just a few words, "With very few exceptions, all activities in the dismantled mills have ceased and their *bateyes* have become ghost towns".[15]

Additional Considerations

More than a decade after the restructuring process started, it appears that the initial predictions of poor industry performance had already became a reality. At the outset, some world sugar specialists reacted with some degree of skepticism concerning a successful outcome.[16] No one, however, questioned the need for restructuring Cuba's sugar agro industry.[17] While the plan implemented appeared to be appropriate, questions about its nature remain unanswered or inadequately addressed. For example: the methodology used in selecting the best lands and most efficient mills to remain in production; the procedure followed for the clustering of lands and mills once the previous selection was completed; how agricultural yields were going to almost double in just 2 years; although 4 million tons appears in several sources, a sugar production goal was never set; diversification efforts lacked a thorough explanation; no concrete plan to regain profitability was set forth (a MINAZ report[18] analyzing the performance of the Basic Units of Cooperative Production in their first 10 years of operation (1993-2003) showed that more than half were unprofitable).

Minister Rosales del Toro stated that having 2.5 million acres available for *organopónicos* and intensive gardens, mixed crops, beef and milk livestock development, and fruits was an enviable goal in today's world.[19] It never happened. I cautioned at that time about an abandonment of the effort after a short period of time, along with skepticism about the Cuban sugar industry's ability to switch

---

14 Peters (2003: 8).

15 Álvarez and Pérez-López (2006: 51).

16 Licht (2002).

17 Álvarez and Peña Castellanos (2001: 91-106).

18 (2003: 7).

19 Varela Pérez (2003).

back to higher levels of output (as is done in Brazil) when world prices called for such a move. Time proved me right, as explained in the following section.

Sugar Industry's Performance
After the 10-million-ton Campaign

Figure 10.1. Cuba's raw sugar production, 1970-2010 (million metric tons).

The graph starts with the disastrous 10-million-ton campaign, when production reached 8.54 million metric tons of raw sugar. The devastating impact of the giant crop translated into an average output of 5.89 million tons in the next seven harvests. It was around that time that Cuba strengthened its commercial relations with the U.S.S.R. and the rest of the socialist bloc and experienced an increase in subsidies while assuming the position of main sugar supplier of the CMEA countries. The average for the next three campaigns reached 7.19 million metric tons. Early in the 1980s, the implementation of the extensive growth model, characterized by the heavy use of modern inputs coming from the European partners, came to the scene. In the next 12 harvests, from 1980-1981 through 1991-1992 (establishment of the Special Period) sugar output averaged 7.52 million tons per year. That period included four harvests with output higher than 8 million tons, very close to those achieved during the 1970 fiasco. From the first harvest that was really impacted by the Special Period (1992-1993) until the campaign prior to restructuring (2001-2002) average throughput in each of the 10 harvests declined to 3.085 million, or to half of the previous period. The remaining eight sugar campaigns took place after the restructuring process, not all under Castro's directives, but because of his policy. What has happened? A dismal average of 1.53 million metric tons per year! During six of those harvests, output was lower than 1.5 million metric tons, production levels comparable to Colonial times, when the island fledging industry surpassed the million tons in 1894 and 1895.[20] All seems to indicate that no change is in sight.

The following quote by Castro, indicates that the decision lacked prior studies and the country started paying the consequences very soon. On August 3, 1994, referring to a comment made by a Delegate to the National Assembly of People's Power (ANPP), Fidel Castro revealed his position concerning the sugar industry.[21] He recalled that 7 million tons had been produced in 1992, and that output had fallen to 4.2 million tons the following year, and to 4 million tons in 1994. He even said that the industry had enough sugarcane to produce the sugar needed but were unable to grind it. Then, he asked a series of critical questions: "What is happening or will happen with that sugarcane? Is there going to be a *surplus?* What are they doing about it? What are the Basic Cooperative Production Units [UBPC] doing? How are the UBPCs performing? How are the UBPCs doing in sugarcane planting? Can we afford the luxury of allowing a single UBPC not fulfilling its sugarcane-planting goals?" Fidel Castro then wondered about the future of the industry. He expressed his concern of production declining from 7 to 4.2 million tons, which would make it difficult to satisfy the country's fuel needs. Then, he asked: "How do we keep the light bulbs burning? How do we import those food items?"

---

20 Thomas (1971: 1562).

21 FL0508182094 Havana Tele Rebelde and Cuba Vision Networks in Spanish 2240 GMT 3 Aug 94 FL0508182094 Havana Tele Rebelde and Cuba Vision Networks Spanish BFN [Address by President Fidel Castro at the evening session of the National Assembly of the People's Power, ANPP, at the Convention Center in Havana -- recorded].

A Final Thought on Sugar

An important change was the way Fidel Castro valued the sugar industry and what it represented for the country. Reading his calculations of the economic value of one *caballería* (13.4 ha or 33.16 acres) planted to sugarcane makes one wonder about him changing his mind and ordering the dismantling of such a productive enterprise. After telling his audience on July 29, 1977 that sugarcane was "a good thing", he went on to prove to them why.[22] Right after recognizing that the national average was between 625 and 750 short tons per caballería, he started the calculations assuming a yield of 1,250 tons, which can yield 150 short tons of sugar and 50 short tons of blackstrap molasses. Dehydrated molasses feed poultry: the 50 short tons represent the equivalent of 45 short tons of corn, which would be an almost impossible agronomic task due to the country's climate. Next, Castro converted the molasses into torula (a yeast), to obtain the equivalent of 11 short tons of soy flour, which also would be almost impossible to get from the soil. Castro added the baggase, used to run the mills and converted the surplus into wood, paper and other derivatives. He then said that he had forgotten that rum was also obtained ("that rum that you consume during the holidays and carnivals also comes from the molasses"), and the alcohol used in the hospitals and … (Remember the Milkmaid and her Pail? In this case, the syndrome reached the level of *delirium tremens*).

For the inquisitive reader: the area devoted to sugarcane production in Cuba encompassed 4.7 million acres at the time Castro made his decision to restructure the industry. If Castro's enthusiasm about the productive potential of one *caballeria* of sugarcane just described were true, a simple multiplication would provide a figure representing the huge opportunity cost involved. The belief held during the life of the Republic that "there is no country without sugar" had already changed under Castro to "and neither with sugar!"

---

22 http://www.cuba.cu/gobierno/discursos/1977/esp/f290777e.html.

Chapter 11

MANAGEMENT EXCEPTIONALISM?

Al animals are equal, but some animals
Are more equal than others.
George Orwell.[1]

The commandment in *Animal farm*, although intended for the communist leadership, applies also to Castro's preference for some projects and his rejection of others. Exceptionalism is the perception that something does not need to conform to normal rules or general principles. Can the term be used to describe agricultural projects where Fidel Castro has not been directly involved in the day-to-day management decisions? Three projects appear to present that characteristic: The Turquino Project, the Baby Chick and the Urban Agriculture movement. Fidel Castro has been conspicuously absent from the leadership of those projects. This chapter explores the existence of a common denominator that could unveil the reasons why.

---

1 (1994: 174).

The Turquino Plan

Origin and Objective

On June 2, 1987, Cuba's Council of State established the Turquino Plan (referring to the highest mountain in the country), following Raúl Castro's initiative.[2] Its main objective was to achieve an integral and sustainable development in the mountainous regions and isolated areas with difficult access, combining harmoniously productive requirements and social development, conservation of nature, strengthening the country's defense, and integrating in their actions the agencies and institutions involved in the process. In 1995, by Decree-Law No. 197, the Executive Committee of the Council of Ministers established the National Planning Commission of Plan Turquino as an inter-agency committee subordinated to the Executive Committee of the Council of Ministers, and composed of the central government agencies with the greatest involvement in the development of the area.

Area Involved

The Turquino Plan covers all four mountainous regions of the country, which constitute about 18% of the total area and are located in 49 municipalities of eight provinces. Its population of 678 207 inhabitants, living in 977 settlements, represents 6% of the country's population and has a density of 77 persons per square kilometer. Close to 81% of their total population resides in the eastern provinces.[3] The work implemented is contained in the evaluations that follow.

---

2 http://es.wikipedia.org/wiki/Plan_Turquino; http://www.cnctv.icrt.cu/noticia/municipio-buey-arriba-m%%C3%%A1s-destacado-en-plan-turquino.

3 http://www.ecured.cu/index.php/Plan_Turquino.

Evaluations

I found two evaluations from outsiders. Antonio Alonso, founder of the independent cooperative movement in Cuba, did the first in 2007.[4] His flat conclusion after two decades of implementation is that of complete failure.

The main objectives of the plan were the recovery of coffee production and the improvement of the living conditions of the rural population, including the repopulation of rural areas. Hundreds of agricultural technicians of all levels of expertise, along with members of the Work Army Youth (EJT), were called upon to enroll. In the Second Front municipality, 50 technicians and 500 recruits arrived. The technicians were located in pairs (males and females) in the Camps with the purpose of establishing families in those rural areas. The young recruits who married residents received some support for housing and purchases of livestock, which included pigs and poultry.

Alonso continued his evaluation stating that, what looked like an attempt by the Cuban government to reverse the traumatic results of a wrong and negative agricultural policy, did not take long to become another failure. Promises went unfulfilled, technicians began to withdraw from the areas, returning to their places of origin or engaging in other work activity. The reactivation of the tourist sector was a great opportunity for many of them, generating a systematic desertion. At the end, all returned to its initial state, deepened in the most absolute neglect.

Of the Turquino Plan settlers only those who have received land in usufruct stayed, which shows that the individual interest over the economic mechanisms is above any political end. It is sad to contemplate in places like Valerio the ruins of driers, pulping houses, housing and shelters for coffee pickers, totally abandoned –infrastructure that existed before 1959.

Alonso concludes that the situation would be different, after 50 years, in the absence of confiscations and forced agricultural collectivization, which killed the sense of belonging and the relationship between the results of the work and the improvement of the living conditions of the rural population.

---

4 The article is entitled "El fracas del Plan Turquino" [The Turquino Plan's failure] and was posted on July 2, 2007, at http://Cuba.Blogspot.com/2007/07/El-fracaso-del -Plan-Turquino.html.

The other evaluation, conducted three years after the previous one, or in 2010, is more comprehensive and contains relevant figures. This is what Olga Mas Tamargo[5] found: 1) Thirty-four percent of housing is in poor conditions, 12% is not electrified and only 85% of those who have power obtain it through the national grid. 2) In the 55% of informal settlements that have access to radio and television, the signal is deficient. Only 52.5% of the settlements have telephone connections. 3) The condition of roads is deplorable and healthcare is difficult because the vehicle fleet for health services is over 20 years old. 4) From 2004-2008 the population of these regions experienced a growth of only 0.6% annually. 5) Rural hospitals have declined from 44 in 2004 to 37 in 2008, and 4 of the latter are in bad shape. The 2008 statistical information reflects very low levels of investment. 6) The 15% of homes damaged by Hurricane Ike are still to be repaired. In Granma province, a proposal to build housing with wood from palm trees and thatched roof is underway.

Information published in the Cuban press of May 2010 appears to support the previous evaluations. Jorge Cuevas Ramos, member of the Communist Party's Central Committee and first secretary of the Party in the province of Holguín, took part in 2009 of the review of the Turquino Plan along with two other government officials. Cuevas Ramos stated, "The excuses that limit the use of the productive potential of the mountains are over. It should start and progress without delay and justifications." The strong statement originated in the sharp decline of coffee production in the areas of the Turquino Plan. As an example, in 1979-1980, output was 1,104,000 coffee cans, while the figure in 2009 was only 271,000 cans.

Mas Tamargo criticizes the low level of investment devoted to these areas, such as 34 million pesos in 2008, which have not been able to improve the livelihood of the people in the Cuban mountains after 23 years.

Production figures show the failure of this gigantic plan when comparing statistics in 2008 with 2004, which show a decrease of 40% in cocoa production,

---

5   The title of the article is "¿Qué pasó con el Plan Turquino?" [What happened with the Turquino Plan?] posted on 17 of May, 2010 at http://cubaout.wordpress.com/2010/05/17/%C2%BFque-paso-con-el-plan-turquino/

of 12% in the production of tubers, and of 22% in vegetables production. As in the rest of the country, all Turquino production is under state control, which sets prices at very low levels.

Pondering about its Exceptionalism

The previous evaluations are very revealing. First, the leadership of Fidel Castro is not a necessary condition to guarantee the plan's failure. Fidel has not been involved publicly in any of the decisions nor has he appeared at any of the celebrations despite his love for gigantomania.

Why did Castro not select this as one of his pet projects in agriculture since he has been involved in almost all of them? The only plausible answer is that the original idea was not his and he could not refuse going along with it for whatever reason. He has also been conspicuously absent from the tens of events related to the Plan in the areas where it operates. Another reason could be his assertion that coffee could also be grown on the plains, and perhaps better than in the mountains. His competitive nature made him avoid a plan based on mountain coffee.

After a long research, I have found a couple of indirect references to the Turquino Plan. During the 25th celebration of the foundation of the enterprise at Los Naranjos, on May 26, 1989, he said:[6] "Also developing strongly enough are the coffee plantations and other crops in the mountains, through the Turquino Plan." That statement came two years after the project was functioning. That has been all to this day, except for a minor reference in another speech. Why did not this gigantic plant get the attention of the commander in chief?

The Baby Chick

Widely publicized in Cuban newspapers at that time, there is a good account in Orozco.[7] Cubans enjoy chickens and eggs. However, chickens eat animal feed, and the latter is imported. Therefore, raising chickens and selling them to the public is costly. Thus, the Cuban government decided to deliver a recently born chicken, already vaccinated against smallpox, to every Cuban to live in their

---

6   http://www.cuba.cu/gobierno/discursos/1989/esp/f260589e.html.
7   (1993: 451-452).

homes and to feed and eventually eat when its weight was appropriate. Instead of taking the urban citizens to the agricultural fields, this time agriculture would go to the urban areas.

This effort started in December 1991 —fifteen months after the official announcement of the Special Period. In an interview with the newspaper *Tribuna de la Habana*, Roberto Borrego, director of Havana's avian enterprise, stated that the program had been such a success that "the population has shown growing interest in acquiring the baby chicks, demonstrated by the constant question: "When are the chicks going to arrive?"

Orozco points out that until March 1992 the Cuban government had sold (yes, they were not free) 1,571,000 baby chicks to the population. Borrego made clear to the newspaper that the chicks would not replace the chicken quota sold under the rationing system.

The reality is that in the small apartments of Havana the baby chicks died soon because the people did not know how to feed them or did not have the proper food, or the chickens became tamed animals like a dog or cat. As with many of the previous plans, the end of the "pollito" approach to mitigate the food problem never became public. Fidel Castro never referred to this plan in a single speech nor is there evidence that he had invented or approved such a ridiculous idea. As opposed to the midget cow project that would take place later in 2004, the failed baby chick plan did not need Fidel Castro's direct involvement.

Perhaps Castro pondered about the project and the numbers turned him against it before implementation: the 1,571,000 baby chicks sold to the same number of households in 1982 needed almost two months to produce some meat. During that time, the family had to provide food and water, perhaps medications, light to warm them up (assume no blackouts) and good cleaning utensils and products to avoid the droppings from becoming part of the house decorations. Fidel would have sold a hen and a rooster (thinking always of his genetic revolution) to make the hen lay eggs that would return more baby chicks. Such arrangement would allow all members of the family to eat a piece of chicken each. However, with the current housing overcrowding, how were they were

163

going to have some privacy to be able to reproduce? (Shhh, shut up Pepito, you are disturbing the birds!) Fidel is a smart leader after all.

The Urban Agriculture Movement

Many agriculturalists and public in general are praising Cuba's efforts in the area of urban agriculture. I feel obliged to discuss it despite Castro's absence from this scenario to avoid bias accusations for excluding an apparent successful plan.[8]

The Special Period witnessed the proliferation of urban agriculture. "The urban gardening movement in Cuba was born out of absolute need and it was spontaneously headed by groups of people with little knowledge about agriculture. Many of the new gardeners were cultivating for the first time."[9] By 1997, the "National Urban Agriculture Group" (GNAU) was established as the leading organization for these efforts.[10]

The intensive gardens (*huertos*) and *organopónicos* are the primary methods of urban cultivation. The structure of the enterprise determines its name: gardens operate on preexisting soil while *organopónicos* operate in raised beds. It is obvious that, due to the poor nature of urban soils, the latter are more popular than the former.

The proliferation of both has been a startling event for a population who devotes a great deal of time to finding food for their families. A survey conducted in 1997 found 7,998 of these gardens in Ciudad de la Habana province, accounting for 37,300 acres.[11] In 2007, the report for the entire Havana province was of 88,700 acres, and over three million acres for the country.[12] The statistics of the previous year for total vegetables and fresh condiments production was of 4.2 million tons for 2006.[13] That would be the equivalent of 82.4 pounds

---

8 This section is based on Altieri et al. (1999); Álvarez (2004a: 146-147); Componioni et al. (2001: 93-110); Koont (2011).

9 Altieri et al. (1999: 133).

10 The GNAU has a complex structure with numerous participating entities (See Koont 2011: 37-39).

11 Companioni et al. (1996).

12 Koont (2011: 30), as taken from a slide presentation by Companioni Concepción.

13 Koont (2001: 165).

per capita.[14] Therefore, these agricultural production units provide a modest, albeit important, contribution to food consumption in urban areas, especially in Ciudad de la Habana province.

It may sound ironic that Fidel Castro has never been involved in urban agriculture at any level. Yet it appears that the initiative represents a modest success compared to the need of the population but a huge one relative to the dismal ending of most of the projects led by the leader of the revolution.

---

14 Cuba's statistical yearbook reports a population of 11,239,043 for 2006 (http://www.one.cu/ aec2011/esp/03_tabla_cuadro.htm).

PART III

THE PARASITISM

Chapter 12

FUNDING THE FOLLIES

There is no dignity quite so impressive, and no one
Independence quite so important, as living within your means.
Calvin Coolidge.[1]

The last chapter of the book explains how Fidel Castro was able to finance so many follies. Although none of the methods is new, Castro appears to have combined and planned the sequence of his sources in a novel manner and in a length of time that has no competitor whatsoever. This chapter

---

1 http://www.searchquotes.com/search/Living_Beyond_Your_Means/

is especially important for the international community because they have become the financial supporters of Fidel Castro's continued string of failed projects.

Financing Butch Cassidy Style
(No Need for the Sundance Kid)[2]

Dumont[3] has stated that Castro's economic errors have cost Cuba dearly. This may be the first time I have to disagree with the famous French agronomist who knew so much about Cuban agriculture and its undisputed architect: No, Mr. Dumont, Castro's economic errors may have imposed costs on the Cuban population at the beginning of the revolution. After that, foreign countries paid his bills. Not only the Soviet Union but also Western countries gave financial support to a leader who was wasting his country's resources in senseless projects with very little probabilities of success.

After digesting all the agricultural follies detailed in this book, the reader may be wondering how has Cuba survived more than fifty years of Castro's misadventures? The answer is simple but unknown by the general public: Fidel Castro used his political adroitness to secure funding from abroad. The process started at the outset of his advent to power and has continued to this day.

It is a historical fact that, when the revolution got in power on January 1, 1959, it found the warehouses full of goods and commodities, the result of a well-functioning economic system. Little by little, as the result of simple arithmetic, when consumption exceeds production, stocks dwindle and the warehouses get depleted. At that point, although explained in ideological terms, Castro decided that other people were going to provide the resources that his policies were unable to create. The history of nationalizations, expropriations and simple

---

2 "Butch Cassidy and the Sundance Kid" is a 1969 American Western film that tells the story of two famous outlaws of the 1890s as they rob banks in the United States and eventually migrate to Bolivia in search of a more successful criminal career. Cassidy is the "affable, clever, talk-ative leader of thir gang; his closest companion is the laconic dead shot Sundance Kid." (http://en.wikipedia.org/wiki/Butch_Cassidy_and_the_Sundance_Kid).
3 (1970: 214-215).

thefts started even before the day he got in power. Although with the passing of time this approach became intertwined with other strategies, it is appropriate to study them separately.

The First Commander and the 8ᵗʰ Commandment

Due to the length and complexity of the process of seizing property from private individuals or corporations in Cuba it is necessary to develop an appropriate framework. Some authors prefer a periodization.[4] Since each period contains several approaches to "free financing," I prefer to separate them by sources (policies affecting specific group of individuals or sectors of the economy).

First Source (1959-1960):
Misappropriated Assets by Batista's Dictatorship

One of the agencies in the first revolutionary Cabinet was the Ministry of Misappropriated Asset Recovery. Its objective was to recover the assets of members or collaborators of the Batista regime, whether they were in Cuba or had fled abroad.

The following numbers provide an idea of the magnitude of the value of the assets transferred to the Cuban government from this group. There were 640 such individuals from the executive, legislative and judicial branches, in addition to governors and mayors whose properties were taken, plus 120 individuals who had benefited from their relations with the dictatorship. The *Gaceta Oficial* published a list of more than 3,000 individuals and corporations confiscated and another 4,000 under investigation.[5] By the end of 1960, the revolutionary government had confiscated more than $25 billion worth of private property owned by Cubans who belonged in this group.[6]

---

4 See, foir example, Anillo-Badia (2011).

5 Anillo-Badia (2011: 84).

6 Lazo (1970: 198-200, 204).

Second Source (1959-1963):
The Land and its Improvements

The first Agrarian Reform Law was enacted on July 17, 1959. A more radical second law came in October 1963. Both pieces of legislation placed most of the arable land in State hands. The resulting socialist versus private sector breakdown of the slightly more than 27 million acres gave 90.2% was in the former and the remaining 9.8% in the latter group.[7]

It is hard to estimate the value of the nationalized properties under the two agrarian reform laws. Part of that amount is included in a section below.

Third Source (1960):
Urban Housing

On October 14, 1960, the Council of Ministers enacted the Constitutional Law of Urban Reform which became an additional text to the Fundamental Law.[8] The law turned 85% of renters into "owners" of the houses they inhabited.[9] I found no data on the number of dwellings, let alone their total value at that time. The entire stock passed to the hands of the regime since the newly created owners had to pay rent for their housing to the government which, in turn, paid a portion to the former owners. The total figure must run in the billions of dollars.

Fourth Source (1960):
Industrial and Banking Sectors

Several Laws enacted in October of 1960, expropriated most assets from Cuban nationals and foreign interests, mainly the United States. The two groups are considered separately.

In lieu of a non-existent official list of the value of the property seized by the Castro regime, it is necessary to use the numbers generated by the Cuban Claim Program of the under the Foreign Claims Settlement Commission of the United States.

---

7 Álvarez (2004a: 44).

8 Álvarez (2000: 103, 121.

9 Instituto Nacional de Ahorro y Viviendas (National Insitute of Savings and Housing), Havana, March 15, 2005.

During the 1966-1972 that the Commission was active, it received a total of 8,816 claims from U.S. nationals: 1,146 from corporations and 7,670 from individual citizens.[10] The 5,911 claims certified were given a value of US$1.8 billion.

Estimates for Cuban-Americans (or, in general, Cuban exiles) have been placed at US$6.9 billion in 1957 values.[11] The figure does not include the value of the properties belonging to Cubans residing in the United States who did not file and those who have remained on the island. Therefore, missing from that total are the industries, factories, sugar mills, and many other belonging to those Cuban nationals. Some of the former values, however, include part of the expropriated land not accounted for above.

Fifth Source: (1961):
Currency Holdings

The measure was simple: get rid ("demonetize") of the old currency in circulation and substitute it with a new one.[12] And, I may add, make a profit in the process.

The official excuse for promulgating Law No. 963 of 1961was that the fugitives from the Batista's dictatorship had taken with them about 424 million of Cuban pesos and deposited them in US banks.

During August 6 and 7 of 1961, most Cuban residents waited in long lines to bring their now old cash and receive 200 pesos per family nucleus of the new currency (for a total de 292 million), with the remaining money going into a bank account to be withdrawn at a rate of 100 pesos monthly. The official historical account seems to have forgotten that the maximum amount allowed per family nucleus was $10,000; the currency beyond that amount was lost by the owners since it could not be deposited in the bank account.

The operation resulted in 724 million pesos surrendered from the assumed 1,187 millions in circulation. Of the remaining 463 million, 424 were assumed to

---

10 1972 FCSC Report.

11 Ashley and Mastrapa (2005: 159).

12 The information appears in EcuRed, an official Cuban source under the heading "Canje de moneda."

be out of the country and the remaining 39 million were said to be in "counter-revolutionary" hands.

At the end of the second day of the exchange, the government came into possession of $487.7 million pesos ($424 million out of the country + $39 million in "counterrevolutionary" hands not exchanged + $24.7 million above the $10,000 limit). The old currency was burned and the missing one was declared worthless. The Cuban government added close to $500 million Cuban pesos to its accounts.

Sixth Source (1968):
Whatever was Left

Castro himself announced the disappearance of the last vestiges of private property during his speech at the University of Havana on March 13, 1968. His lengthy discussion included the results of investigations on small kiosks, self-employment activities, and other practices that, according to him, did not lead to building socialism, especially the existence of 955 bars in the capital. His speech led the way to what is called "the revolutionary offensive."[13]

Hours after his speech, the offensive to eliminate the private sector started in every corner of Cuba. The following month, the official newspaper *Granma* published the results:[14] A total of 55,636 small businesses, mostly worked by one or two persons, were confiscated. Included were 11,878 small markets; 3,130 butcher shops; 3,198 bars; 8,101 establishments for the selling of processed food; 6,653 dry cleaners; 3,643 barbershops; 1,188 shoe repair shops; 4,544 auto mechanic shops; 1,598 craft shops, and 3,345 carpentry shops.

The immediate result was a huge increase of the deterioration of the economy that had started several years before and an extraordinary decline in the availability of food and services. It is impossible to put a value figure to such a massive confiscation. For simplicity purposes, if we assume the value of each of these small businesses at 10,000 Cuban pesos, the total worth of the confiscation would be over 555 million. If a more realistic (albeit conservative) figure of an average value of 20,000 Cuban pesos, the total figure would be over 1billion Cuban pesos.

---

13 His speech can be read at http://www.cuba.cu/gobierno/discursos/1968/esp/f130368e.html.
14 The list has been taken from Espinosa Chepe (2012).

Deterioration of the Stock of Assets

The cash obtained from the change in currency was soon spent and the stock of capital goods started deteriorating almost since the very beginning and accelerated with the passing of time. Obviously, Fidel Castro paid no attention to the concept of depreciation and the replacement of depreciated assets.

Wear and tear —an important part of depreciation— occurs even when an asset is used with care and proper maintenance. A normal practice is to set up an account to provide for the replacement of the depreciated asset; for example, a piece of machinery, once its economic life has ended. The concept also applies to buildings. Cuban cities are a living example of the second law of thermodynamics: "objects will get messier and more worn down over time unless energy from the outside world is used to fix them."[15] The rubble on the streets from crumbling buildings seems to echo Castro's words in the first year of the revolution:[16] "What is ideal? That everybody has his house, and then it would be worth travelling through some of our cities and that at least the facades are painted; if not, we will be forced in the future to demolish all the buildings of this poorly constructed Havana as to make them new again."

---

15 http://en.wikipedia.org/wiki/Wear_and_tear.
16 Speech of 16 March 1959: http://www.cuba.cu/gobierno/discursos/1959/esp/f160359e.html. See, for example, the documentary "Havana, the new art of making ruins" (http://cinemaguild. com/mm5/merchant.mvc?Screen=PROD&Store_Code=TCGS&Product_Code=2258).

He did not have to do that terrible job. Time did it for him. Buildings in Havana and the rest of the country only need a light rain to collapse, adding rubble to streets and sidewalks.

Borrow → Default → Forgive → Borrow

The Case of the Soviet Union

The relationship between the Soviet Union and Cuba began taking shape after the United States broke commercial and diplomatic relations with the latter in 1960 and 1961, respectively. With the passing of time, the U.S.S.R. subsidized the Cuban economy at a rate estimated at between US$5 and US$6 billion per year.

Table 12.1. Foreign aid from the Soviet Union to Cuba, 1960-1990.

| Period | Repayable Loans (Debt) | | | Nonrepayable price subsidies | Total aid |
| | Trade deficit | Development | Subtotal | | |
	US $ million				
1960-1970	2,083	344	2,427	1,131	3,558
1971-1975	1,649	749	2,398	1,143	3,541
1976-1980	1,115	1,872	2,987	11,228	14,215
1981-1985	4,046	2,266	6,312	15,760	22,072
1986-1990	8,205	3,400	11,605	10,128	21,733
Total	17,098	8,631	25,729	39,390	65,119[a]

[a] It excludes military aid, reported as $13.4 billion in 1960-85.

Source: Calculated from several sources by Mesa-Lago (1993a: 148).

The Case of Western Countries

While the Castro regime was receiving subsidies and loans from the Soviet Union and the rest of the Socialist Bloc, it was also borrowing from Paris Club member countries and whatever other country would extend credit to the island.

Table 12.2. Cuba's total foreign debt after-Soviet era, 2008.

Rank	Creditor (Country)	Amount (US$)
1	Venezuela	11.367 billion
2	Spain	3.200 billion
3	China	3.170 billion
4	Japan	2.775 billion
5	Argentina	1.967 billion
6	France	1.856 billion
7	Romania	1.236 billion
8	Russia (post Soviet)	1.149 billion
9	Iran	656 million
10	Panama	425 million
11	Germany	411 million
12	Mexico	400 million
13	Italy	371 million
14	Brazil	350 million
15	United Kingdom	342 million
16	Vietnam	297 million
17	Czech Republic	278 million
18	Belgium	231 million
19	Netherlands	149 million
20	Austria	95 million
21	Canada	94 million
22	Trinidad & Tobago	30 million
23	Uruguay	30 million
24	Sweden	26 million
25	Denmark	14 million
26	Portugal	5 million
27	Switzerland	3 million
	Undisclosed	751 million
TOTAL		31.681 billion

Source: European Union, *Cuba Country Strategy Paper and National Indicative Programme for the period 2011-2013*, 24 March 2010. Annex VIII: Debt Sustainability Analysis.

A more recent estimate puts Cuba's external debt at US$41.1 billion at the end of 2011 and a projection of US$23.5 at the end of 2014.[17] The lower figure is due to the reported write off and renegotiation of Cuba's debt with Russia, which is the subject of the following section.

---

17   Luis R. Luis, "Cuba's external debt problem: Daunting yet surmountable," ASCE BLOG, http://www.ascecuba.org/blog/post/2013/12/18/Cubas-External-Debt-Daunting-Yet-Surmountable.aspx.

Forgiveness and Borrowing Again

For many different reasons, creditors have a tendency to write off part of the debt owed to them and either forgive or renegotiate the rest. After that process, the former debtor starts the cycle all over again.

The Cuban regime made an attempt in the 1980s to renegotiate its debt with Western countries. In 1982, the Cuba requested the renegotiation of the medium-term debts from its creditors and the postponement of these payments for a period of ten years, including a three-year grace period.[18] The attempt was unsuccessful..

After defaulting in the mid-1980s, Cuba and some of its creditors engaged in a process of "debt restructuring" that has added billions of dollars to the Cuban government's balance sheet. In October 2013, Russia and Cuba announced they had reached an agreement whereby Cuba committed to pay US$3.2 billion over a 10-year period in exchange for Russia forgiving the rest of a US$32 billion debt --$20 billion plus service and interest.[19] The agreement is assumed to open the way to new investment and trade and, there is little doubt, a new cycle of credit Cuba-Russia. The agreement has also changed Cuba's standing with the Paris

---

18 Martínez-Piedra and Pérez (1986: 32-33), from a report by Cuba's National Bank.

19 See report by foreign correspondent in Havana Marc Frank, dated December 9, 2013, titled "Exclusive: Russia signs deal to forgive $29 billion of Cuba's Soviet-era debt —diplomats."

Club.[20] Since Russia is now a member of the Paris Club, by removing a large part of its debt, it has strengthened Cuba's ability to gain concessions from other Paris Club members, now that the debt is smaller, or about US$15.5 billion at the end of 2012.

Russia is not the only country that has granted concessions to Cuba. According to the same report, in 2010 China restructured the US$9 billion that Cuba owed that country. In 2012, it was Japan. Under the agreement, Japan forgave 80% of the US$1.4 billion debt, with the remainder to be paid over 20 years. In 2014, it was Mexico's turn, which pardoned 70% of a US$478 debt Cuba accumulated in the late 1990s; the remaining US$140 million is to be paid over a 20-year period. Mexico immediately announced it would expand Cuba's credit line to purchase Mexican goods and services.[21]

More countries are bound to follow. Cuba's inefficient economic model is not likely to bring about larger output to pay for the upcoming new credits. Yet these countries insist in granting more and more to the ruined Caribbean nation. Why?

In a provocative book published in 2009 about eight centuries of financial folly, Reinhart and Rogoff ridicule the excuse used along those years to justify this financial stupidity: "This time is different." Since this book is concerned with the Cuban case, the obvious reply to that prediction must be the question: Is it?

With Butch Cassidy out of the picture, his brother has implemented a series of economic reforms aimed at mitigating the dismal state of Cuba's economy.[22] Cuba is obviously in desperate need of cash to finance those reforms.

Enter the Sundance Kid.

---

20 The Paris Club is an informal group of 19 permanent creditor governments that includes Canada, France, Germany, Japan, Russia, the United Kingdom and the United States plus a number of smaller European countries (Austria, Belgium, Denmark, Finland, Ireland, Italy, Netherlands, Norway, Spain, Sweden and Switzerland) and Australia. There are also 12 associate members.

21 Cubastandar.com: Cuban Business and Economic News.

22 See Mesa-Lago (2012) and Mesa-Lago and Pérez-López (2013).

The erasing of part of the Cuban foreign debt and the recent negotiations to extend fresh money to the Cuban regime by opening new credit lines will not be enough. As stated above, Raúl Castro's regime is now paying cash for the food purchased in the United States. The possibility of having those purchases financed by the American taxpayer in the case of default is a tempting proposition for Cuba to engage in negotiations to end the embargo.

The reasoning is simple: The lifting of the sanctions would open the possibility for Cuba of taking advantage of the benefits offered by the Export-Import Bank of the United States, the official export credit agency of the United States. Ex-Im Bank's mission is to assist in financing exports of U.S. goods and services to international markets.[23] The Ex-Im Bank provides working capital guarantees (pre-export financing); export credit insurance; and loan guarantees and direct loans (buyer financing).

That possibility has already been mentioned in the media.[24] Some have expressed concerns about selling "boundless goods and services to the Cuban government on credit, with their receivables being guaranteed by the U.S. taxpayer." The probabilities of default are great indeed, in which case the American taxpayer would get stuck with Cuba's bills.

---

23 http://www.exim.gov/about/
24 https://thelastwire.wordpress.com/2014/05/22/the-myth-of-the-cuban-embargo/

AFTERWORD

*W*hen Fidel Castro was in Mexico preparing his invasion of Cuba, he wrote what was called the Manifesto No. 1 of the 26 of July Movement to the people of Cuba. The Manifesto, obviously written by Castro himself, has a date of August 8, 1955, and the following excerpt fits the theme of this book:

> [Has] not Batista jeopardized the credit of the country for 30 years? Has not the public debt increased to more than 800 million pesos? Is there not a deficit of more than 100 million? Are not the monetary reserves of the nation pledged to foreign banks in a desperate search for money?... Can one play like that with the destiny of a nation?[1]

As the last thought, without the need for writing an Epilogue, it is convenient to recall a dialogue between Fidel Castro and a resident of Moa, Oriente province, during a visit he paid on August 26, 1966.[2] Castro was talking about how his government had lowered rents but could not build houses for every family: "...houses cannot be drawn from a hat like a circus' magician, like Mandrake,[3] who draws rabbits from a hat..." (As shown in chapter 1, that was

---

1 The text can be read in Dirección Política (1979: 129-134).

2 http://www.cuba.cu/gobierno/discursos/1966/esp/f260866e.html.

3 Mandrake here refers to the main character of a newspaper comic strip that portrays a magician whose work was based on an unusually fast hypnotic technique (http://en.wikipedia.org/wiki/Mandrake_the_Magician).

not his thinking on February 16, 1959, when Castro promised: "I can tell you that, with the passing of time, the Savings and Housing Institute will build all the houses the country needs."[4])

One could not agree more with Castro. He could not draw rabbits (his rabbit project failed), or cows (large and midget), hens and chickens, and every other type of animals, fruits and vegetables from the Cuban soil, more fertile than the magician's hat. Expanding Birán to cover the Cuban archipelago ended in a complete failure, leaving a debt many times larger than the one he attributed to Batista.

No, Fidel Castro is not Mandrake. Cuba is not an expanded Birán. Moreover, the management of the agricultural sector should be in the hands of qualified professionals.

When Fidel Castro started to feel better after a long convalescence, he decided to devote himself to the task of saving the human race by sharing his wisdom in the printed press via a column entitled *"Reflexiones del Comandante en Jefe"*. He has warned about local conflicts that could lead to a nuclear disaster that would do away with life on this planet [Remember the 1962 missile crisis?]. From time to time, he offers his knowledge on agricultural topics, especially his bias against the so-called energy crops, or discovers things he had not noticed before. That was the case with his Reflection entitled *"La alimentación y el empleo sano"* [Feeding and the healthy job] ending as usual with his signature and the time : 17 June 2012 at 2:55 pm... He was pushing *moringa*[5] production in Cuba!

The text reads: "The conditions are present for the country to start massively producing *Moringa Oleifera* and *Morera,* which are inexhaustible sources of meat, egg and milk, silk fibers that can be spinned for handicrafts and are capable of providing work, on the shade and well paid, regardless of age or sex".

One could hear the exclamations: "Oh, no; not again!" However, do not fear. He is not coming back to lead the agricultural sector. He is not even returning to his beloved Birán, where the family house is experiencing its third refurbishing

---

4   http://www.cuba.cu/gobierno/discursos/1959/esp/c160259e.html.

5   *Moringa* is a tree that originated in India but grows quickly in many types of environments. The leaves are rich in protein, vitamin A, vitamin B and vitamin C.

at the time of this writing. In that land (hopefully on the proper side of the fence), the family vault serves as the final resting place of his parents Ángel and Lina. Even from Havana, Fidel can hear the chorus of a song made popular by Pototo and Filomeno in the mid-1950s: *ENTREN QUE CABEN TRES...* [Come in, there is room for three...] This time he cannot touch the fruits of his parents' orange grove as he did on Christmas Eve of 1958 on his way to absolute power. They are not there anymore. They disappeared like most of his follies.

Appendix

NEGATIVE ENVORONMENTAL IMPACTS

It is worthwhile indicating that the main responsibility for the brutal destruction of the environment lies with the consumer societies.
Fidel Castro.[1]

Fidel's Special Plans not only were responsible for huge economic losses but also for inflicting an incalculable damage to the agricultural environment. Cuba's natural resources will never be the same. This Appendix provides a general overview of such damages in selected areas.

Soil Erosion

In addition to natural phenomena (rains, rivers and winds), modern agricultural practices are the main culprits of soil erosion.[2] In Cuba, the problem accelerated with the implementation of the state extensive growth model in agriculture during the 1980s (see chapter 7). The COMARNA[3] estimated at that time that over 19 million acres out of a total land area of 27.2 million acres, or about 70%, suffered from some degree of erosion.[4] Although erosion is more evident in

---

1 Speech at the United Nations Conference onf the Environment and Development, Rio de Janeiro, June 12, 1992, at http://www.cuba.cu/gobierno/discursos/1992/ing/f120692i.html.

2 Núñez-Jiménez (1968) wrote this interesting book for farmers explaining what soil erosion is, why it is a problem and the means to alleviate it.

3 (1991: 11-12).

4 Espino (1992: 330).

the mountains, it is also considerable in Cuba's most fertile and relatively flat regions.[5]

Culprits: The state extensive growth model of the 1980s; Water works project; San Andrés de Caiguanabo; The "Che" Guevara invading brigade; Cayajabos terraces; The Turquino plan.

Soil Compaction

The physical properties of the soil as well as the use of machinery and equipment contribute to soil compaction. The tremendous increase in the use of heavy machinery and equipment associated with the implementation of the state extensive growth model is a well-known fact.[6] According to COMARNA[7] soil compaction affects almost 4 million acres of agricultural land in Cuba.[8]

Culprits: The state extensive growth model of the 1980s; Water works project; The "Che" Guevara invading brigade.

Soil Salinity and Acidity

Excessive irrigation may produce or aggravate soil salinity, as may also inadequate irrigation and the excessive use of fertilizers. The COMARNA[9] reports that 10% of Cuba's total surface area suffers from salinization.[10] Some specialists put that figure at 32% of agricultural lands.[11] The COMARNA[12] meanwhile reports land affected by acidification at 28.5% of all agricultural lands, or 4.38 million acres.

Total land area affected by degradation problems at the end of the 1990s was broken down as follows:[13] Erosion = 10,451,322 acres; Compaction = 3,953,686

---

5 Díaz-Briquets and Pérez-López (2000: 92).
6 Álvarez and Messina (1992).
7 (1991: 15).
8 Sáez (1997: 45).
9 (1991: 11-12).
10 Espino (1992: 330).
11 Sáez (1997: 46).
12 (1991: 53).
13 Adapted from Sáez (1997, Table 7).

acres; Salinization = 1,928,904; Drainage = 6,671,845 acres; Acidification = 2,800,939 acres.

Cuba's Ministry of Science and Technology, assisted by consultants from the Netherlands, produced a Report in 1997 that corroborates the problems identified above. Affected land amounts to 26.44 million acres, which represents 60% of the national territory. The Report emphasizes the degree of desertification and deforestation that have put Cuba on the way to becoming a desert.[14]

Culprits: The state extensive growth model of the 1980s; Water works project; The torula project.

Water Resources

The supply of water for the agricultural sector has always been a priority of the Cuban regime and the focus of many of Fidel's Special Plans. The establishment of the National Institute of Hydraulic Resources (INRH) as early as 1962 reflects Castro's objective that "not a single drop of water be lost, that not a drop of water reach the sea… that a single stream or river not be dammed."[15]

Wotzkow,[16] who states that they are responsible for extensive flooding during the hurricane season and for the desert-like scenario that dominates the rural areas during the dry season, has criticized the building of an excessive number of dams. Several scientists[17] have posed serious questions about the entire water works project.

The ambitious dam construction program has resulted in several negative impacts, such an increase in the extraction rate of underground water, a high degree of contamination of waters in aquifers, and growth in land areas with salinization.[18] The Paso Seco dam, located in the capital area, has the objective of retaining the waters of the Almendares River. Because of its small capacity and

---

14 Solares (2010: 92).

15 El paisaje (1982: 52).

16 (1998: 131-137).

17 Díaz-Briquets and Pérez-López (2000:118-119, 124, 125, 133). See also Wotzkow (1998: 131-137).

18 Díaz-Briquets and Pérez-López (2000).

inadequate construction, there is need to constantly discharge its waters, which results in the flooding of several neighborhoods in Havana.[19]

Furthermore, agricultural and animal production in 1989 was generating around 9 million tons of solid residues and about 27 million cubic meters of liquid residues per year.[20] In addition to the increase of a waste disposal problem, contamination of waters intensified.

A Cuban scientist[21] identified torula yeast wastewater as one of the most significant sources of stream and soil pollution in Cuba. The quantity of wastewater exceeded 30,000 cubic meters, with an average 20 grams per liter of solids and very high acidity coming from the country's torula yeast plants. At present, that pollution must have decreased due to fewer plants functioning.

Culprits: The state extensive growth model of the 1980s; Water works projects; The genetic revolution; The torula project.

Marine Resources
There are hundreds of kilometers of virgin beaches and shore, which we are now connecting, where possible, to the mainland.
Fidel Castro.[22]

The building of *pedraplenes* (causeways) have affected in a negative manner not only Cuba's marine resources but also those on adjacent lands. These causeways block the movement of intra-coastal waters, increasing contamination and destroying coastal and marine habitats.[23] According to Wotzkow,[24] they have brought an enormous ecological damage, including the loss of marine species, nearby forests, and agricultural lands. Just in the Sabana-Camagüey sub-archipelago, the *pedraplenes* affect over 1,760 square kilometers of fragile ecosystems,

---

19 http://www.naturalezacubana.org/localidades/habana.html.

20 Atienza Ambou et al (1992: 13).

21 Sánchez Hernández (1992). See also Oro (1992: 55)..

22 Speech of May 10, 1990 at http://www.cuba.cu/gobierno/discursos/1990/esp/f100590e.html.

23 Espino (1992: 335).

24 (1998: 138-141).

leading to the destruction of natural fauna and flora and the creation of lagoons of stagnant, polluted water devoid of wildlife.

The destruction starts in nearby hills with the removal of the original vegetation in order to extract the rocks for the construction of the causeway. After building the causeway, thousands of fish float dead in the vicinity. The logical consequence is the displacement of the anglers because of the disappearance of most marine species.

A Cuban scientist[25] from the Center for Environmental Studies and Services in Las Villas has compiled the best-documented evidence of major negative impacts of *pedraplenes* around the world. Cayo Coco is listed in ten of the 18 categories: increase in salinity; loss of biodiversity; depletion of fishing resources; changes in the zoning of phytobenthos; increase in water temperature; increase in the time of recharging bay waters; loss of habitats; changes in hydraulic regimes; diminishing larvae dispersion; and damage to mangrove swamps and marine pastures.

The damage described above only refers to Cayo Coco. To picture the entire impact one would have to multiply it several times over to account for the likely damage inflicted to the areas surrounding these causeways, built in the least appropriate manner. Wotzkow[26] estimates that the income generated by one of the hotels in a year, would not be enough to pay for the ecological damage inflicted to one foot of beach in Cayo Coco.

Culprits: The *pedraplenes* (causeways); Water works project; Zapata swamp plan

Deforestation

Mangroves are trees that grow on salt water. They are like a protective barrier of coasts, important in allowing the confluence of fresh water and salt water to take place. Although they are part of the shoreline, instead of marine resources they are classified as forestry.

---

25 Quirós Espinosa (2013).
26 (1998: 143).

There are several mangrove regions in Cuba. Development projects conducted in several of those regions have had a negative impact on the natural vegetation.[27] According to Wotzkow, mangroves account for 26% of total forest resources and have suffered from over exploitation, the main victim being the Zapata Swamp area due to the many project executed there.[28] The other culprit is the water works project; dams and reservoirs interrupt the natural flow of water from the land to the coast and they are killing the mangroves.

It is appropriate to recall at this point that, on the dawn of December 2, 1956, the *Granma* yacht, carrying Fidel Castro and his 81 men, was approaching the Cuban shoreline. Castro landed in the mangroves of Los Cayuelos region, converting the landing in a true nightmare. It took them two hours walking in the moody waters to reach Cuban soil. It would have been much easier today.

The Turquino Plan led to migrant agriculture (slash and burn), and consequently to the greatest damage to the country's most important natural forests. Between one harvest and the next and, aggravated by rains and erosion, the top soil disappeared just one year after the clearing.[29]

The "Che" Guevara Invading Brigade destroyed around 445,000 acres of natural forestry between 1967 and 1969. Most of them are now unproductive areas displaying signs of desertification.[30] On December 24, 1967 Castro congratulated the Brigade for having cleared 140,472 acres in Oriente and stated that there were 1,952,982 acres more to clear in the rest of the country.[31]

Culprits: The *pedraplenes* (causeways); Water works project; Zapata swamp plan; The Turquino plan; The "Che" Guevara invading brigade.

---

27   Díaz Briquets and Pérez-López (2000:157).
28   COMARNA (1991: 9).
29   Wotzkow (1998: 160).
30   Cepero (2004: 4).
31   http://www.cuba.cu/gobierno/discursos/1967/esp/f241267e.html.

List of Credits

Cover: © 2014 by Virginia Gifford

Chapter 1

- Ration booklet - (http://caimitoyyo.blogspot.com/2009/09/la-libreta-de-racionamiento-en-mi.html).
- Food line – (http://veusnoticias.com/cualquier-parecido-con-la-realidad-es-pura-coincidencia-asi-controlan-al-pueblo-cubano-en-las-colas-para-comprar-alimentos-la-foto/).
- 3 cows in AC: http://octavocercoen.blogspot.com/2009_11_01_archive.html; and also http://www.cubademocraciayvida.org/web/article.asp?artID=22841.
- Cuba plus IoP (Wikimedia Foundation).

Chapter 2

- Sign in Biran (Photoshelter_Purchase ivr1qEF19xM).

Chapter 4

- FC3 (notiultimas.com: http://notiultimas.com/digital/index.php?option=com_content&view=article&id=21862:putin-se-reunira-con-fidel-castro-durante-su-gira-por-america-latina&catid=40:america-latina&Itemid=62; http://www.caribdirect.com/decisions-on-cuba-rooted-in-politics-not-principle/.

Chapter 5

- Casa-de-San-Andres (http://cubaaldescubierto.com/?p=4524).
- Zapata swamp (Google maps).

- Mayari Pinewoods (AIN Holguin province: http://www.cubadebate.cu/fotorreportajes/2009/12/18/el-salto-del-guayabo-en-pinares-de-mayari-uno-de-los-mas-altos-de-cuba/#.U5zPzSjb4pF.
- House Pinewoods (http://cubaaldescubierto.com/?p=4524).

Chapter 7
- Rosafe Signet (Canada's *Holstein Journal*)
- FC and UB (http://www.juventudrebelde.cu/multimedia/fotografia/ubre-blanca/ubre-blanca/) (Unknown source).
- Midget cow (http://baracuteycubano.blogspot.com/2006/03/desmontando-las-mentiras-del-castrismo.html).
- Crossing (Academia de Ciencias de Cuba 1988: 70).
- FC tv 10 million (*Diario Granma*, February 15, 1970).
- Causeway billboard (http://primiciadiario.com/wp-content/uploads/2012/05/CUB4.jpg).
- Causeway plus car (Dollar Photo Club 59850178).

Chapter 12
- Horse wagon (Dollar Photo Club 3003808).
- Bldg D FC_598251 (Dollar Photo Club).
- FC with US$ (Archive photo).

Bibliography

Academia de Ciencias de Cuba. 1988. *Ciencia, técnica y revolución*. La Habana: Editorial José Martí.

Albarrán, Antonio. 1998. *Don Quixote de la Mancha, Miguel de Cervantes Saavedra*. Madrid: Grafalco.

Alfonso, Pablo. 2013. *Fidel y Raúl – Delirios y fantasías*. Madrid: Fundación Hispano Cubana.

Altieri, Miguel A., Nelso Companioni, Kristina Cañizares, Catherine Murphy, Peter Rosset, Marin Bourque and Clara I. Nichols. 1999. "The greening of the "barrios": urban agriculture for food security in Cuba," *Agriculture and Human Values* 16 (1999): 131-140.

Álvarez, José. 1990. "A chronology of three decades of centralized economic planning in Cuba." *Communist Economies* 2:1 (2000): 101-125.

Álvarez, José. 2003. "Natural disasters and Cuba's agricultural performance: is there a correlation?" *Cuba in Transition* 13 (2003): 227-233.

Álvarez, José. 2004a. *Cuba's Agricultural Sector*. Gainesville, FL: University Press of Florida.

Álvarez, José. 2004b. "The current restructuring of Cuba's sugar industry". *EDIS Document FE472*, Food and Resource Economics Department, Florida

Cooperative Extension Service, Institute of Food and Agricultural Sciences, University of Florida, January. (Revised, August 2009. Reviewed, June 2013). http://edis.ifas.ufl.edu/fe472.

Álvarez, José and William A. Messina, Jr. 1992. Potential exports of Florida agricultural inputs to Cuba: fertilizers, pesticides, animal feed, and machinery. *International Working Paper IW92-33*, International Agricultural Trade and Policy Center, Food and Resource Economics Department, University of Florida, Gainesville, Florida, December.

Álvarez, José and Ricardo A. Puerta. 1994. "State intervention in Cuban agriculture: Impact on organization and performance." *World Development* 12:11 (1994): 1663-1665.

Álvarez, José and Lázaro Peña Castellanos. 2001. *Cuba's sugar industry*. Gainesville, FL: University Press of Florida.

Álvarez, José and Jorge F. Pérez-López. "The Restructuring of Cuba's Sugar Agroindustry: Impact on Rural Landscape and Communities." <u>Journal of Rural and Community Development</u> 2:1 (2006), pp. 44-58.

Álvarez Tabío, Pedro. 2003. *Celia – ensayo para una biografía*. La Habana: Oficina de Publicaciones del Consejo de Estado.

American Psychiatric Association. 2000. *Diagnostic and statistical manual of mental disorders (DSM-IV-TR-4th edition. Tex Revision)*. Washington, DC: American Psychiatric Association.

Anillo-Badía, Rolando. 2011. Outstanding claims to expropriated property in Cuba. *Cuba in Transition* 21 (2011): 83-96.

Aranda, Sergio. 1975. *La revolución agraria en Cuba*. México: Siglo XXI Editores, 6th ed.

Arenas, Alberto, Kris Bosworth and Hardson Kwandayi. 2006. Civic Service Through Schools: An International Perspective. *Compare* 36:1 (March), pp. 23-40.

Ashby, Timothy and Tania Mastrapa. 2005. Taxation of Cuban confiscated assets after property claims settlements: Issues for taxpayers and the U.S. government. *Cuba in Transition* 15(2005):157-166.

Associated Press. 2002. Reconvierten ingenio azucarero cubano con financiamiento externo (Cuban sugar mill is restructured with foreign financing). Havana, Cuba, November 8.

Atienza Ambou, Aida. Anicia García Álvarez and Oscar U. Echevarría Vallejo. 1992. Repercusiones medioambientales de las tendencias de desarrollo socioeconómico en Cuba (Environmental repercusiones of socioeconomic development tendencies in Cuba). La Habana: Instituto Nacional de Investigaciones Económicas.

Baloyra, Enrique. 1993. Socialist transitions and prospects for change in Cuba. In Baloyra and Morrids (Eds.), *Conflict and change in Cuba*, pp. 38-63.

Baloyra, Enrique A. and James A. Morris. (Eds.) 1993 *Conflict and change in Cuba*. Albuquerque, NM: University of New Mexico Press.

Barkin, David. 1980. Confronting the Separation of Town and Country in Cuba. *Antipode* 12:3 (December), pp. 31-40.

Benjamin, Medea, Joseph Collins and Michael Scott. 1986. *No Free Lunch - Food and Revolution in Cuba Today*. New York, NY: Grove Press.

Betto, Frei. 1985. *Fidel y la religión – Conversaciones con Frei Betto*. La Habana: Oficina de Publicaciones del Consejo de Estado.

José Álvarez, PhD.

Blanco, Katiuska. 2003. *Todo el tiempo de los cedros – Paisaje familiar de Fidel Castro Ruz*. La Habana: Casa Editorial Abril.

Blanco Castiñeira, Katiuska. 2008. *Ángel, la raíz gallega de Fidel*. La Habana: Casa Editora Abril.

Blanco Castiñeira, Katiuska. 2012. *Fidel Castro Ruz, Guerrillero del tiempo – Conversaciones con el líder histórico de la Revolución Cubana*. Primera Parte. Tomo I. Blog Cuestionatelotodo, de José Luis Forneo.

Blanco Castiñeira, Katiuska. 2013. *Fidel Castro Ruz, Guerrillero del tiempo – Conversaciones con el líder histórico de la Revolución Cubana*. Primera Parte. Tomo II. Blog Cuestionatelotodo, de José Luis Forneo.

Borrego Díaz, Orlando. 1965. Problemas que Plantea a la Industria una Zafra de 10 Millones de Toneladas de Azúcar. *Cuba Socialista* 5:44 (April), pp. 10-30.

Brean, Erin. 2004. Personalistic political leadership in Castro's Cuba. *Leadership Review* 4 (Fall 2004): 132-137.

Bunck, Julie Marie. 1994. *Fidel Castro and the quest for a revolutionary culture in Cuba*. University Park, PA: The Pennsylvania State University Press.

Cabrera, René. 2012. *Agua de rosas*. Miami, FL: Alexandria Library.

Carnoy, Martin. 1981. Educational Reform and Economic Development in Cuba: Recent Developments. *Education Resources Information Center*. Http://eric.ed.gov/ERICWebPortal.

Castro, Fidel. 1969. Speech to the members of the Revolutionary Armed Forces who will participate in the 10-million-ton harvest, MINFAR Theater, November 4. http://www.cuba.cu/gobierno/discursos/1969/esp/f041169e.html

Castro, Fidel. 1970. Report on 10-million-ton sugar harvest by TV and radio, May 21. http://lanic.utexas.edu/la/cb/cuba/castro/1970/19700521.

Castro, Fidel. 1990. *Ciencia, Tecnología y Sociedad, 1959-1989.* La Habana: Editorial Política.

Castro, Fidel. 1991. *Ciencia, Tecnología y Sociedad, 1988-1991.* La Habana: Editorial Política.

Castro, Fidel. 1992. *Ecología y desarrollo: sección temática, 1963-1992.* La Habana: Editorial Política.

Castro, Fidel and Ignacio Ramonet. 2006. *Fidel Castro. My life – A spoken autobiography.* New York, NY: Scribner.

Castro, Juanita. 2009. *Fidel y Raúl, mis hermanos. La historia secreta – Memorias de Juanita Castro contadas a María Antonieta Collins.* Doral, FL: Aguilar.

Castro Figueroa, Abel R. 2011. *El país de la ciguaraya.* Bloomington, IN: Palibrio.

Casuso, Teresa. 1961. *Cuba and Castro.* New York, NY: Random House.

Cepero, Eudel Eduardo. 2000. La situación ambiental de Cuba al finalizar el siglo XX. *Cuba in Transition* 20(2000): 173-189.

Cepero, Eudel Eduardo. 2004. *Environmental Concerns for a Cuba in Transition.* Miami, FL: Institute for Cuban and Cuban-American Studies, University of Miami, Cuba Transition Project.

Chonchol, Jacques. 1963. Análisis crítico de la reforma agraria cubana. *El Trimestre Económico* Vol. XXX (1), No. 117, Enero-Marzo, pp. 69-143.

COMARNA. 1991. Informe nacional a la Conferencia de Naciones Unidas sobre Medio Ambiente y Desarrollo Rural, Brasil 1992: Resumen Ejecutivo (National report to the United Nations conference on environment and development, Brazil 1992: Executive summary). Havana, Cuba.

Companioni, Nelso, Egidio Páez, Yanet Ojeda and Catherine Murphy. 2001. La agricultura urbana en Cuba. In Fernando Funes, Luis García, Martin Bourque, Nilda Pérez and Peter Rosset, Eds. *Transformando el campo cubano – Avances de la agricultura sostenible*. La Habana: Asociación Cubana de Técnicos Agrícolas y Forestales.

Current Developments in the Cuban sugar industry. 2000. *Sugar y Azúcar* 95:11, pp. 18-19, 22-23.

Cuzán, Alfred G. 1999. Fidel Castro: A Machiavellian prince? *Cuba in Transition* 9(1999): 178-190.

Cuzán, Alfred G. 2004. Franco's Spain and Castro's Cuba: Parallels and contrasts. *Cuba in Transition* 14(2004): 181-195.

Díaz-Briquets, Sergio and Jorge Pérez-López. 2000. *Conquering Nature: The Environmental Legacy of Socialism in Cuba*. Pittsburgh, PA: University of Pittsburgh Press.

Dirección Política de las FAR. 1979. *De Tuxpán a La Plata*. La Habana: Editorial Orbe.

Draper, Theodore. 1969. *Castroism – Theory and practice*. New York, NY: Praeger Publishers.

Dumont, René. 1970. *Cuba: Socialism and Development*. New York, NY: Grove Press.

Dumont, René. 1971. *Cuba, ¿Es Socialista?* Caracas: Editorial Tiempo Nuevo, 2nd ed.

Duncan, W. Raymond, 1994. Cuba-U.S. relations and political contradictions in Cuba. In Baloyra and Morris (Eds.), pp. 215-241.

El Paisaje se Transforma (The landscape changes). 1982. *Voluntad Hidráulica_*19, pp. 52-58.

El sistema de dirección y planificación de la economía en las empresas [The sistem of economic management and planning of the enterprises]. 1981. La Habana: Editorial de Ciencias Sociales.

Enríquez, Laura J. 1994. *The question of food security in Cuban socialism.* Berkeley, CA: International and Area Studies, University of California.

Espino, María Dolores. 1992. Enrironmental deterioration and protection in socialist Cuba. *Cuba in Transition* 2(1992): 327-342.

Espinosa Chepe, Oscar. 2012. La ofensiva revolucionaria de 1968, 44 años después. *Cubaencuentro/cuba*March 27, at http://www.cubaencuentro.com/cuba/articulos/la-ofensiva-revolucionaria-de-1968-44-anos-despues-275328.

Ezrow, Natasha and Erica Frantz. 2011. *Dictators and dictatorships – Understanding authoritarian regimes and their leaders.* New York, NY: The Continuum International Publishing Group.

Fagen, Richard R. 1965. Charismatic authority and the leadership of Fidel Castro, *The Western Political Quarterly* 18:2 Part 1 (June 1965): 275-284.

Figueroa, Max, Abel Prieto and Raúl Gutiérrez. 1974. *La Escuela Secundaria Básica en el Campo: Una innovación educativa en Cuba.* Paris: Editorial de la Unesco.

Frank, Marc. 2002a. Cuba will downsize sugar industry by 50 pct - minister. *Transmission and Distribution World,* June 18. http://tdworld.com/ar/agriculture_cuba_downsize_sugar/index.htm.

Frank, Marc. 2002b. Castro moves to calm Cuban sugar industry's worries. *Forbes,* October 22. http://www.forbes.com/business/newswire/2002/10/22/rtr761254.html.

Franqui, Carlos. 1988. *Vida, aventuras y desastres de un hombre llamado Castro.* Barcelona: Editorial Planeta.

Gall, Norman. 1971. How Castro Failed. *Commentary* 52:5 (November), at http://www.normangall.com/artigos/How_Castro_Failed_pdf.

Galvin, Benjamin, David A. Waldman and Pierre Balthazard. 2010. Visionary communication qualities as mediators of the relationship between narcissism and attributions of leader charisma. *Personnel Psychology* 63:3 (Autumn): 509-537.

Gasperini, Lavinia. 2000. *The Cuban education system: lessons and dilemmas.* Washington, DC: The World Bank.

Gastón, Melchor W., Oscar A. Echevarría and René F. de la Huerta. 1957. *Por qué reforma agraria.* (Why agrarian reform). Serie B: Apologética. Folleto no. 23. Buró de Información y Propaganda. Agrupación Católica Universitaria, La Habana, Cuba.

Geyer, Georgie Anne. 1991. *Guerrilla prince.* Boston, MA: Little, Brown and Co.

Gifford, Lauren. 2010. The numbers diet: food imports as economic indicators. *Cuba in Transition* 20 (2010): 47-51.

Ginsbergs, George (Ed.). 1987. *A calendar of Soviet treaties, 1974-1980.* Hingham, MA: Kluwer.

González, Edward and David Ronfeldt. 1986. *Castro, Cuba, and the world.* The Rand Corporation.

Gutelman, Michel. 1967. *La agricultura socializada en Cuba.* México: Ediciones Era.

Hagelberg, G.B. and José Alvarez. 2006. Command and countermand: Cuba's sugar industry under Fidel Castro. *Cuba in Transition* 16 (2006): 123-139.

Halperin, Maurice. 1974. *The rise and decline of Fidel Castro.* Berkeley, CA: University of California Press.

Halperin, Maurice. 1992. Fidel's power to disrupt. In Hugh M. Hamill (Ed.) *Caudillos – Dictators in Spanish America*, pp. 316-324.

Hamill, Hugh M. (Ed.) 1992. *Caudillos – Dictators in Spanish America.* Norman, OK: University of Oklahoma Press.

Heredia, J., Marisol Muñiz, O. López and J. Ly. 2004. Una reseña corta sobre 45 años (1959-2002) en el desarrollo de la porcicultura cubana. *Revista Computarizadora de Producción Porcina* 11:1 (2004): 5-22.

Hermans, H.J.M. 1998. Meaning as an organized process of valuation. In P.T.P. Wong and P.S. Fry (Eds.) *The human quest for meaning: A handbook of psychological and clinical applications* (pp. 317-334). Mahwah, NJ: Erlbaum.

Herrera, Raúl. 1965. Problemas que Plantea a la Agricultura una Zafra de 10 Millones de Toneladas. *Cuba Socialista* 5:43 (March), pp. 1-23.

Hoffmann, Bert. 2009. Charistmatic authority and leadership change: Lessons from Cuba's Post-Fidel Succession. *International Political Sciemce Review* 30:3 (June 2008): 229-240.

Hoffman, Bert and Laurence Whitehead. (Eds.) 2007. *Debating Cuban exceptionalism.* New York, NY: Palgrave Macmillan.

House,, R.J. and J.M. Howell. 1992. Personality and charismatic leadership. *Leadership Quarterly* 3(1992): 81-108.

Hubbard, R. Glenn and William Duggan. 2009. *The aid trap – hard truths about ending poverty.* New York, NY: Columbia University Press.

Jenks, Leland H. 1928. *Our Cuban Colony: A Study in Sugar.* New York, NY: Vanguard Press.

Kling, Merle. 1962. Cuba: A case study of a successful attempt to seize political power by the application of unconventional warfare. *Annals of the American Academy of Political and Social Sciences* 341 (May): 42-52.

Koont, Sinan. 2011. *Sustainable urban agriculture in Cuba.* Gainesville, FL: University Press of Florida.

Laird, Roy D. and Betty A. Laird. 1970. *Soviet communism and agrarian revolution.* New York, NY: Penguin.

Latell, Brian. 2012. *Castro's secrets- The CIA and Cuba's intelligence machine.* New York, NY: palgrave macmillan.

Lazo, Mario. 1968. *Dagger in the heart: American policy failures in Cuba.* New York, NY: Twin Circle Publishing Co.

Licht, F.O. 2002. Cuba seeks to revamp its sugar industry. *International Sugar and Sweetener Report* 134 (20): 309, 311-314.

Lockwood, Lee. 1990. *Castro's Cuba, Cuba's Fidel.* Boulder, CO: Westview Press.

Lockwood, Lee. 1992. Fidel Castro speaks on personal power. In Hugh M. Hamill (Ed.) *Caudillos – Dictators in Spanish America*, pp. 292-315.

Lutjens, Sheryl L. 1998. Education and the Cuban revolution: A selected bibliography. *Comparative Education Review* 42:2, pp. 197-224.

Marques, Joan F. 2007. On impassioned leadership: A comparison between leaders from divergent walks of life. *International Journal of Leadership Studies* 3:1 (2007): 98-125.

Martínez-Piedra, Alberto and Lorenzo L. Pérez. 1996. External debt problems and the principle of solidarity: The Cuban case, *Cuba in Transition* 6(1996):23-41.

McGuire, Randall H. 2008. Chapter 6: Marxism. In Bentley, R. Alexander, Herbert D.G. Maschner and Christopher Chippindale (Eds.) *Handbook of Archaeological Theories*. Lanham, MD: Altamira Press, pp. 73-93.

McGuire, Patrick and Karen Vocke. 1988. Cuba. In Rebecca Marlow-Ferguson and Chris Lopez (eds.) *World Education Encyclopedia*, Vol. I, pp. 297-304. Detroit, MI: Gale Publishing.

Mesa-Lago, Carmelo. 1973. Tipología y valor económico del trabajo no remunerado en Cuba. *El Trimestre Económico* XL (159), Julio-Septiembre, pp. 679-711.

Mesa-Lago, Carmelo. (Ed.) 1974. *Revolutionary change in Cuba*. Pittsburgh, PA: University of Pittsburgh Press.

Mesa-Lago, Carmelo (Ed.) 1993a. *Cuba after the cold war*. Pittsburgh, PA: University of Pittsburgh Press.

Mesa-Lago, Carmelo. 1993b. The economic effects on Cuba of the downfall of socialism in the USSR and Eastern Europe. In Mesa-Lago, (Ed.) *Cuba after the cold war*, pp. 133-196.

Mesa-Lago, Carmelo. 2012. *Cuba en la era de Raúl Castro: reformas económico sociales y sus efectos.* Madrid: Editorial Colibrí.

Mesa-Lago, Carmelo and Jorge F. Pérez-López. 2013. *Cuba under Raúl Castro: Assessing the reforms.* Boulder, CO: Lynne Rienner Publishers.

MINAZ. 1999. *Diversificación – Bases del Proceso de Perfeccionamiento del Complejo Agroindustrial Azucarero* (Diversification - Basis of the process of improvement of the agroindustrial complex). La Habana, Cuba: Ministry of Sugar.

MINAZ. 2003. Informe Resumen de los Resultados Alcanzados por las UBPC Cañeras en el Período 1993-2003 (Summary report of the sugarcane UBPCs results in the 1993-2003 period). La Habana, Cuba: Ministry of Sugar and National Syndicate of Sugar Workers, October 31.

Mitchell, Rex C. and Don Rossmoore. 2001. Why good leaders can't use food advice. *Journal of Leadership Studies* 8:2 (Fall): 79-105.

Montaner, Carlos Alberto. 1994. *Víspera del final: Fidel Castro y la revolución cubana.* Editores Globus (http://www.hacer.org/pdf/Montaner09.pdf).

Nova González, Armando. 1993. Cuba: ¿Modificación o Transformación Agrícola? (Cuba: Modification or agricultural transformatioon?). La Habana: Instituto Nacional de Investigaciones Económicas. Mimeo Report.

Nova González, Armando. 1994. La reorganización de la agricultura en Cuba: Factor clave en la estabilización económica. (The reorganization of agriculture in Cuba: the key factor in the economic stabilization). La Habana: Instituto Nacional de Investigaciones Económicas. Mimeo Report.

Núñez-Jiménez, Antonio. 1968. *La erosión desgasta a Cuba.* La Habana: Instituto del Libro.

Oro, José R. 1992. *The poisoning of Paradise — The environmental crisis in Cuba*. Published in the United States by the Endowment for Cuban American Studies of the Cuban American National Foundation.

Orozco, Román. 1993. *Cuba Roja: Cómo Viven los Cubanos con Fidel Castro*. Madrid: Información y Revistas.

Orwell, George. 1994. *Rebelión en la granja*. Barcelona: Ediciones Destino.

Otero, Lisandro. 1960. *Cuba: Z.D.A.* Havana: Ediciones R.

Padilla, Art, Robert Hogan and Robert B. Kaiser. 2007. The toxic triangle: Destructive leaders, susceptible followers, and conducive environments, *The Leadership Quarterly* 18 (2007): 176-194.

Pardo Llada, José. 1988. *Fidel y el "che"* Barcelona: Plaza & Janes Editores.

Partido Comunista de Cuba. 1991. Resolución sobre el desarrollo económico del país. *Granma*, October 17, p. 3.

Pérez-López, Jorge F. 1991. *The economics of Cuban sugar.* Pittsburgh, PA: University of Pittsburgh Press.

Pérez-López, Jorge F. and José Álvarez. 2005. *Reinventing the Cuban sugar agroindustry.* Lanham: Lexington Books.

Peters, Philip. 2003. Cutting losses: Cuba downsizes its sugar industry. Washington, DC: Lexington Institute, December. http://www.lexingtoninstitute.org/cutting-losses-cuba-downsizes-its-sugar-industry.

Proyecto El Partido de la Unidad, la Democracia y los Derechos Humanos que Defendemos - V Congreso del Partido Comunista de Cuba. 1997. *Granma*

Internacional. Edición Digital, La Habana. Http://ourworld.compuserve.com/homepage/MHEC/PCCSC.HTM.

Quirk, Robert E. 1993. *Fidel Castro.* New York, NY: W.W. Norton & Co.

Quirós Espinosa, Ángel. 2013. Experiencias hodroecológicas en el diseño del pedraplén de Caibarién, *Ingeniería Hidráulica y Ambiental* 34: 2 (mayo-agosto): 62-72.

Raffy, Serge. 2003. *Castro, el desleal.* Doral, FL: Santillana USA Publishing Co.

Regalado, Antero. 1965. Los pequeños agricultores y el plan azucarero para 1970. *Cuba Socialista* 5:48 (August), pp. 36-50.

Reinhart, Carmen M. and Kenneth S. Rogoff. 2009. *This time is different: Eight centuries of financial folly.* Princeton, NJ: Princeton University Press.

Reyes, Gerardo. 2002. Castro planea clonar a la vaca Ubre Blanca. *El Nuevo Herald,* May 22, p. 4-A.

Rieff, David. 1996. Cuba refrozen: defiance and dollarization." *Foreign Affairs* (July-August), pp. 62-76.

Robinson, John Charles and Víctor Galán Saúco. 2010. *Bananas and Plantains.* Cambridge: CAB International.

Roca, Sergio. 1994. Reflections on economic policy: Cuba's food program." In Jorge F. Pérez-López (ed.) *Cuba at a Crossroads - Politics and Economics After the Fourth Party Congress.* Gainesville, FL: University Press of Florida, pp. 94-117.

Romeu, Emma. 1997. *Los dioses tosen (Reportajes de medio ambiente) México-Cuba: 1986-1997.* Morelia, Michoacán: Universidad de Michoacán.

Ronet, Jorge. 1987. *La mueca de la paloma negra*. Madrid: Editorial Playor.

Rosales del Toro, Ulises. 2002. Intervención del Ministro del Azúcar a los Embajadores Extranjeros en Cuba Sobre la Restructuración del MINAZ (Oral presentation of the Minister of Sugar to foreign ambassadors in Cuba about MINAZ's restructuring). La Habana, December 5. Mimeo Report.

Rosenthal, Seth A. and Todd L. Pittinsky. 2006. Narcissistic leadership. *The Leadership Quarterly* 17(2006): 617-633.

Ruscoe, Gordon C. 1975. Moral education in revolutionary society." *Theory and Practice* 14:4 (October), pp. 258-263.

Sáez, Héctor R. 1997. Resource degradation, agricultural policies and conservation in Cuba. *Cuban Studies* 27 (1997): 40-67.

Sáenz, Tirso and Emilio G. Capote. 1989. *Ciencia y tecnologí en Cuba.* La Habana: Editorial de Ciencias Sociales.

Sánchez Hernández, E.P. 1992. Torula yeast wastewater treatment bt downfall anaerobic filters. *Bioresource Technology* 40:2 (1992): 163-166.

Santayana, George. 1905. *Life of reason, reason in common sense*. New York, NY: Charles Scribner's Sons.

Sartre, Jean-Paul. 1961. *Sartre on Cuba*. New York, NY: Ballentine.

Solares, Andres L. 2010. *Cuba – the disaster of Castro's revolution*. Miami, FL: Xlibris.

Sondrol, Paul C. 1991. Totalitarian and authoritarian dictators: a comparison of Fidel Castro and Alfredo Stroessner. *Journal of Latin American Studies* 23: 8 (October 1991): 599-620.

Sosik, John J. 2000. The role of personal meaning in charismatic leadership. *Journal of Leadership Studies* 7:2(Spring): 60.

Suárez, Andrés. 1967. *Cuba: Castroism and Communism, 1959-1966.* Cambridge, MA: The M.I.T. Press.

Suárez, Andrés. 1974. Leadership, ideology, and political party. In Mesa Lago (Ed.) *Revolutionary change in Cuba*, pp. 3-21.

Szulc, Tad. 1986. *Fidel: A critical portrait.* New York, NY: William Morrow and Company.

Thomas, Hugh. 1971. *Cuba: the pursuit of freedom.* New York, NY: Harper and Row.

Thomas, Hugh. 1977. *The Cuban revolution.* New York, NY: Harper & Row.

Varela Pérez, Juan. 2003. Restructuración Azucarera: El Compromiso de Dar Uso a las Tierras que Pasan a Otros Cultivos (Sugar restructuring: The commitment to use the lands transferred to other crops). *Granma,* October 25, 2003. http://www.granma.cu.

Viera, Félix Luis. 2002. *Un Ciervo Herido.* San Juan: Editorial Plaza Mayor.

Voisin, André. 1959 (English translation in 1988). *Grass productivity.* Washington, DC: Island Publishers.

Wilson, L.L., P.J. LeVan, and R.E. Todd. 1993. Haller livestock/forage farm grazing systems. *Pasture Profit* (November): 2-3.

Wotzkow, Carlos. 1998. *Natumaleza Cubana.* Miami, FL: Ediciones Universal.

Zimbalist, Andrew and Claes Burdenius. 1991. The organization and performance of Cuban agriculture. In Michael J. Twomey and Ann Helwege (Eds.)

Modernization and stagnation – Latin American agriculture into the 1990s. New York, NY: Greenwood Press, pp. 233-260.

Zumaquero Posada, Ovidio, Lucía Santana Díaz and Alberto Siles Denis. 1991. Drenaje parcelario: una metodología de evaluación económica. *Cuba Económica* 1:2, pp. 134-149.

Zúñiga, Jesús. 2000. Cubam minister of agriculture blames embargo for deficiencies. *CubaNet* (http://www.cubanet.org/CNews/y00/jul00/20e7.htm).

Index

Author's Biographical Sketch

José Álvarez was born in Antilla, Oriente, Cuba in 1940. At the age of 10, his parents sent him to a religious boarding school in Santiago de Cuba, the provincial capital. Months later, Fulgencio Batista and a small group of military officers took power by force and started a dictatorship that would last almost seven years. Despite his age, he opposed the new regime since the first day and enrolled in clandestine organizations. When Fidel Castro founded the "26 of July Revolutionary Movement" in 1955, he became a member until it was disbanded by Castro himself after taking power in 1959. Almost three years later, he dropped out of Law School, resigned his position and applied for permission to leave the country. In early February 1969, he was able to travel to the United States with his wife and their 5-year-old daughter. They went to Gainesville, Florida, where he graduated with a Ph.D. in food and resource economics from the University of Florida in 1977, becoming a member of its faculty. After a productive academic career that included over 300 publications, more than 50 presentations in national and foreign events, and numerous grants and awards, José Álvarez retired in 2004, receiving the title of Emeritus Professor. He founded the project "Rethinking the Cuban rebellion of 1952-59" (http://josepepinalvarez.com). Some of the 16 books he has published, have received an equal number of national and international awards including Florida Book Awards, International Latino Book Awards, London Book Awards, Nashville Book Awards, New Generation Indie Book

Awards, Readers Favorite Awards Contest, and several from Editorial Voces de Hoy. For his work on Cuban agriculture, he received the "National Honor Award for Superior Service"", the highest honor conferred by the United States Department of Agriculture to an agricultural researcher. He lives in Wellington, Florida, with his wife Mercy, his son Alejandro and daughter-in-law Monika, and his grandchildren Alexis Monique, Ricardo Julián and Niko Enrique.

www.ingramcontent.com/pod-product-compliance
Lightning Source LLC
Chambersburg PA
CBHW070801280326
41934CB00012B/3008